Allison Robicelli

111 Places in Baltimore That You Must Not Miss

Photographs by John Dean

emons:

For Richard Gorelick, Beth Hawks and Lou Catelli,
the Holy Trinity of lunatics who took us in and made this home.

© Emons Verlag GmbH
All rights reserved
© Photographs by John Dean, except:
page 22: David Iden (Annex Theater)
page 34: Mary Gardella (Baltimore School of the Arts)
page 78: Vincent Vizacher (Fluid Movement)
© Cover motif: shutterstock.com/Opas Chotiphantawanon
Design: Eva Kraskes, based on a design
by Lübbeke | Naumann | Thoben
Maps: altancicek.design, www.altancicek.de
Printing and binding: CPI – Clausen & Bosse, Leck
Printed in Germany 2017
ISBN 978-3-7408-0158-8

Did you enjoy it? Do you want more?
Join us in uncovering new places around the world on:
www.111places.com

Foreword

To paraphrase E. B. White, there are three types of city people. The natives see the city as a birthright, an identity, a place that they inadvertently take for granted. The outsiders see it from afar as little more than a place that has minimal bearing on their lives. The transplants, however, are the people who discover themselves in that city as a part of some sort of grander quest they simply must pursue. I was the first kind: a native New Yorker who loved my hometown but considered the "magical" as profoundly normal. I was an outsider to Baltimore, a city I'd only seen in the news, painted as a post-apocalyptic wasteland by the media and shows like *The Wire*. But then I went to see Baltimore for myself. Within an hour, I desperately wanted to be the third kind: a transplant, who lives in constant awe of the city that surrounds her, the city I now proudly call home.

Uncovering Baltimore is an endless treasure hunt. The history buff in me can't get enough of its old buildings, relics, and stories that go back to the earliest days of colonization. My soul is fed by the electric art scene. The human in me has fallen in love with the people, who are almost too wonderful for words. Theirs is a city that's been repeatedly kicked when it was down, a scrappy underdog that's been counted out too many times.

The people of Baltimore are strong and resilient, facing their challenges head on. They band together to create beauty, to change the way we think about rebuilding the broken pieces of our country. They are proud of their city because they know in their hearts that Baltimore may just be the best city in America. I would have to agree.

Baltimore's nickname is Charm City, and it has stolen my whole heart. If you give it a chance, I guarantee it will steal yours, too.

111 Places

1__1307 Park Avenue

The tragic home of Zelda & F. Scott Fitzgerald

The most iconic couple of the Jazz Age arrived in Baltimore in 1932, though not under happy circumstances. The once glamorous Zelda had been diagnosed with schizophrenia two years prior and sought outpatient treatment at the Henry Phipps Psychiatric Clinic at Johns Hopkins. The move seemed to do her well, as within the first six weeks of treatment she wrote her first, and only, novel, *Save Me the Waltz.* The following year they moved to this Bolton Hill row house, which would become the final home they would share as a couple.

Zelda began taking painting classes at the Maryland Institute College of Art. She wrote a play, *Scandalabra*, which was produced in that summer by the Vagabond Players, a theatrical company still located in Fell's Point. The reviews were negative, and shortly after, her mental condition deteriorated, and she was committed to a sanitarium in New York. When she returned to the Phipps clinic the following year, her condition had worsened. She would spend the rest of her life living primarily in mental institutions, with brief, unsuccessful periods of respite.

Scott developed an affinity for alcohol at a young age, and during the zenith of his celebrity in the Roaring Twenties, he was known to be a lousy drunk who often publically embarrassed himself. As Zelda's mental health deteriorated, his fortunes gone, and his debt worsening, he sank ever deeper into the throes of alcoholism. Seeking a comeback, having not published a novel in a decade, he released *Tender is the Night* in 1934, a semi-autobiographical tragedy, which he considered his greatest work. Sadly, though now considered a masterpiece, it was initially met with scathing reviews and poor sales.

In 1936, Scott was forced to leave this address due to his dire financial situation. Their 15-year-old daughter Scottie was sent to boarding school. Zelda never returned home from the sanitarium.

Address 1307 Park Avenue, Baltimore, MD 21217 | Hours Unrestricted | Tip Named one of the best bars in America by *Esquire* magazine, Mount Royal Tavern (1204 W Mount Royal Avenue, Baltimore, MD 21217) is the dive bar you wish was in your neighborhood. A hot spot for college students, the bar's cheap beer is complimented with high art: the ceiling is a flawless replica of Michelangelo's Sistine Chapel, painted by an alumnus of Zelda Fitzgerald's school, MICA.

2__ The 2 O'Clock Club
The hottest blaze in burlesque

In the 1920s, the burlesque circuit was booming, and Baltimore's stages were a must-play for any burgeoning A-lister. The section of East Baltimore Street that (hilariously) stands across the street from police headquarters became known as "The Block," full of thriving clubs such as the Gayety and the Chanticleer. It was the 2 O'Clock Club that launched the career of Blaze Starr, the woman who would bring the art form to its highest heights.

Fannie Belle Fleming, a teenage runaway, began stripping age 15. Three years later in 1950, she moved to Baltimore and began working at the 2 O'Clock Club, learning the art of burlesque. Her quick wit and knack for comedy were as much of a draw as her flaming red hair and Lamborghini curves, and she soon became the club's headlining act. Her trademark act was called "The Exploding Couch," where she would feign such uncontrollable sexual excitement that smoke would come shooting out from between her legs, and satin flames would start blowing from the cushions. She became known as, "The Hottest Blaze in Burlesque."

A 1954 profile in *Esquire* magazine made her a national star overnight, and soon she was earning over $1,500 a week ($13,000 today) to play the world's top burlesque houses. She was embroiled in one the greatest political sex scandals in history, having a torrid affair with Louisiana Governor Earl Long. Paul Newman's 1989 movie *Blaze* tells the story.

Instead of flocking to Hollywood like Gypsy Rose Lee, Starr stayed in Baltimore, where she eventually bought the club, becoming the only female business owner on the block. She owned it until the 1970s, when burlesque had almost died out and The Block became a den of sleaze and crime. Blaze Starr might be long gone, but the neon sign from the 2 O'Clock Club still dangles high over East Baltimore Street, a reminder of the woman who was once the biggest star in town.

Address 414 E Baltimore Street, Baltimore, MD 21202, +1 (410)783-2656 | **Hours**
Mon, Tue, Wed & Fri 10am–8pm | **Tip** Burlesque is back in a big way in Charm City.
Grab a show at the Windup Space (12 W North Avenue, Baltimore, MD 21201,
www.thewindupspace.com), or check out the *City Paper*, Baltimore's alternative weekly
newspaper, for events; it's rare you'll find a weekend without a good old-fashioned
striptease on the calendar (www.citypaper.com).

3 __ 337 East Hamburg Street
Ghosts in the garage

One block south of Federal Hill Park lies a tiny road that ends on a cliff overlooking the harbor. Amidst the brick row homes is a clapboard house with a simple slant roofed structure that has been divided into apartments. In time, residents learn that their building was once a prison for Confederate spies during the Civil War, and the parking pad was the site of many executions.

Shortly after the riots on Pratt Street (see ch. 81) that claimed the first casualties of the war, Brigadier General Benjamin F. Butler, commander of the Eighth Massachusetts Regiment, came to secure Baltimore. It was imperative that the Union Army have safe access to Washington, DC. With the major railroads passing through Baltimore, any future uprisings by Southern sympathizers needed to be averted. Butler intended to secure Baltimore for the Union and punish those who had fought against the cause.

With 1,000 men in two trains, Butler quickly established an alliance with the men at Fort McHenry and commanded his men to set up station on Federal Hill. The next morning, he sent out a declaration that Baltimore was under martial law with his troops in charge of preserving order, all munitions meant to aid the South would be seized, and all flags and symbols of the Confederacy were to be stripped from the city.

It would be a few days still before the military had their command organized. Shortly after the occupation, Fort McHenry became the official home for all prisoners of war. This did not prevent several men involved in the riots from being arrested immediately. All were brought to the basement of 339 East Hamburg, where General Butler had temporarily taken residence. He stood on the balcony to watch their executions by firing squad in the courtyard below, effectively sending a message to those who wished to instigate further violence: the Union Army was now in control of Baltimore.

Address 337 East Hamburg Street, Baltimore, MD 21230 | **Hours** Unrestricted | **Tip**
Federal Hill's military days are long behind it – is now used as a public park that offers one
of the best views in the city. Take it all in while sitting beside the Civil War cannons that
were used to protect the harbor.

4 Al Capone's Cherry Tree

Danger and dignity in a pre-penicillin age

Notorious mobster Al Capone was finally taken down in 1931 by an elite squad of federal agents nicknamed "The Untouchables" and shipped off to Alcatraz Prison to serve a sentence for tax evasion. Upon his release in 1939, Capone, one of the most powerful mobsters who had ever lived, had become untouchable himself.

When Capone first moved to Chicago as a mob enforcer in 1909, he oversaw security at a brothel, where he contracted syphilis. By 1920 it had become a curable disease, but for unknown reasons, Capone declined treatment. Upon entering prison, his condition went on the record, and after 13 years of ignoring his malady, a significant amount of brain damage had occurred. His writing became incomprehensible; he was barely able to interact with other inmates. Capone's mental condition declined rapidly during his time at Alcatraz, and he spent the final year of his sentence confined to the prison hospital with severe brain damage.

Upon his release, Capone's people wanted him transferred to the leading hospital for treatment of advanced stage tertiary syphilis: Johns Hopkins. The hospital board decided they would not accept him because of his reputation. He was referred instead to nearby Union Memorial Hospital, where he commanded the entire fifth floor, not only for his protection, but also so there would be room for his massive entourage. He spent five weeks at the hospital, and then relocated to the home of a Maryland police sergeant while he spent several months receiving outpatient treatment.

The doctors were able to extend his life, but the damage had been done: Capone's evaluation showed he had the mental capacity of a child. He was cognizant enough, however, to show his gratitude and gifted the hospital with two weeping cherry trees. One tree still remains, a testament to the compassion exhibited within the halls of Union Memorial Hospital.

Address 201 E University Parkway, Baltimore, MD 21218, +1 (855)633-0199,
www.medstarunionmemorial.org | Hours Unrestricted | Tip Close by on the corner of
Canterbury Road and West 39th Street, you'll find the exquisite Ambassador Apartments
building, a pre-war gem with a hidden surprise inside the lobby: the Ambassador Dining
Room, a superlative Indian restaurant many say is the most beautiful in Baltimore
(3811 Canterbury Road, Baltimore, MD 21218).

5 __ Al Capone's Legit Office
Straight as an arrow

Al Capone was a son of New York City who hit it big in Chicago and ended up in Alcatraz. Baltimore always seems to get edged out of the conversation, likely because it was the city that bookended his life. His only stop between leaving prison and dying in seclusion were two years being treated for syphilis at Union Memorial Hospital in North Central Baltimore (see ch. 4). But before that, before Alcatraz, before the gambling and bootlegging and murder, there was Alphonse Gabriel Capone, professional bookkeeper.

Having never completed his formal education, Capone had few employable skills save for one – number crunching, learned by helping run the books for the loan sharking, prostitution, opium trafficking, and number running operations back in New York. In 1919, he found a clerical job at an above-board construction company run by Italian immigrant Peter Aiello and showed up in Highlandtown each morning in a suit and tie. He quickly became a valued employee. It wasn't the high-rolling lifestyle he had been accustomed to, but it appeared that Capone was relishing his "normal" life with his wife and child. Then, back in Brooklyn, his father died suddenly of a heart attack at age 54, leaving behind Capone's mother and his eight siblings. No one is certain what his motivation was, but his father's death also meant the end of his attempts to be a respectable citizen. Shortly after the funeral, Capone told his boss that he had big opportunities available to him in Chicago, and Peter Aiello lent him $500 to follow them.

Capone never forgot this favor. Years later, when he was running the entire show in Chicago, he got wind of his old boss coming to town for an engineer's convention. To express his gratitude he threw Aiello a parade, which marched down the streets of Cicero, with thousands of spectators cheering his name and showering him with confetti.

Address 3700 Gough Street, Baltimore, MD 21224, +1 (410)276-6787, www.dipasquales.com | Hours Mon–Sat 9am–6pm | Tip DiPasquale's itself is known as the best Italian grocery in the city, so you can understand why Peter Aiello would have put his offices above it – if not for the easy answer to "what's for lunch?" then at least for the smells wafting upstairs… The locals say that you *must* order the Meatball Chub with a side of arancini, but honestly, you can't go wrong with anything.

6_Alexander Brown & Sons Building

Follow the money

If you were asked to locate the first investment bank in the United States, you'd probably be inclined to point to New York City, or maybe Boston or Philadelphia. But once again you'd need to turn your eye to the City of Firsts, where Alexander Brown laid one of the cornerstones of the American financial system back in 1800.

Brown arrived from Ireland at the age of 36, choosing the port of Baltimore to launch a small linen-importing business. The company quickly grew, and soon he owned a fleet of clipper ships. He revolutionized American commerce by slashing the shipping times between major coastal markets. His firm organized the first Initial Public Offering (IPO) in the U.S., financing the Baltimore Water Company. Brown continued financing the infrastructure of America, financing the first railroad, the Baltimore & Ohio. One could argue that the blueprints for America's growth into an economic superpower were created because Alexander Brown financed them.

His influence did not stop with his own bank. In 1810 he brought his four sons aboard as partners, who soon expanded the Brown empire. William Brown moved to Liverpool and founded Brown, Shipley & Co.; George and John formed Brown Bros. & Co. in Philadelphia; and James went to New York to open a satellite office. All of these institutions are still standing over 200 years later.

The building at 135 East Baltimore Street was built in 1901, which was decades after Alex Brown and his four sons passed on, but their institutions continued to thrive. A series of mergers has taken them away from their former headquarters, but it has not stopped them from continuing the vital work of building American business: they recently played major roles in the IPOs of companies such as Starbucks, Oracle, and Microsoft.

Address 1 South Street, Baltimore, MD 21202, +1 (410)727-1700 | Hours Unrestricted |
Tip If you really want to eat like a local, skip the crabcakes and go to Lake Trout
(227 E Baltimore Street, Baltimore, MD 21202). Despite the name, it doesn't serve only
trout, but fried fish of whatever species fits a working-class budget (whiting and catfish are
popular choices). Check out Hip Hop Fried Fish & Chicken, and make sure you order a
Half & Half to wash it down.

7 Annex Theater

A world of pure imagination

Some of the most exciting, adventurous, and experimental works in modern theater are being performed in vacant lofts and hidden spaces of Baltimore.

The Annex Theater was never meant to be polished, or even professional. Founded in 2008 inside a dilapidated warehouse next to a cemetery, it was meant to be a place specifically for non-theater artists — a space to cultivate experimental work that was not constrained within the traditional boundaries of the theater. Sharing a home with musicians, artists, and other members of the DIY scene, the Annex quickly absorbed creatives across all disciplines, and a new, strange breed of theater was born that was distinctly Baltimorean.

There are no rules, so there is no way to know what to expect when you visit. They've performed complex science-fiction plays, operas, westerns, complete abstractions and, occasionally, a reinterpretation of a classic. Their ultimate goal: to produce work that breaks molds and causes theatergoers to forget that the concept of a mold ever existed. The company solicits original works from all over the world, giving a stage to playwrights who hate rules, who use their total freedom to push the envelope as far as they'd like. The seasons are intentionally designed to reject consistency at all costs, juxtaposing styles and thematic elements to challenge both audiences and the theater scene as a whole. Companies are intentionally assembled to pit actors and directors with unique creative desires against each other, so that the conflicts that occur in development bring new and unexpected outcomes, seeking beauty in awkwardness, creating new definitions of convention.

The theater scene in Baltimore continues to grow. Seek out Single Carrot, Iron Crow, or just contact the Annex and ask them what to see. The company is only nine years old, but they've already redefined all the rules.

Address 219 Park Avenue, Baltimore, MD 21201, +1 (443)228-6745, www.baltimoreannextheater.org | Hours Check website for current performance schedule | Tip The Annex is a part of the Bromo Arts District, one of three such districts in the city. Every institution is worth a visit, but there's something special about the historic Bromo Seltzer tower - a landmark that has been converted into artist studios (21 S Eutaw Street, Baltimore, MD 21201, www.bromoseltzertower.com).

8 — Arabber Preservation Society

Keepin' it old school

For centuries, goods were sold by men who peddled around in horse-drawn carts called "arabbers." The name (pronounced AY-rubber) comes from an old London slang term "street Arab," which referred to the fact that these merchants would drive their horse-drawn food carts all over the city. This practice became obsolete long ago, and Baltimore is the only city in America where arabbers still exist, largely thanks to the Arabber Preservation Society, which was created in 1994 to support the arabbers' horse stables.

Arrabing was a job that was easier to get into than most, provided you were good at the hustle. Jobs were hard to come by in times where the population boomed but industry had not caught up. Arabbers visited every neighborhood to sell local produce, dairy, and Chesapeake Bay seafood. Most factory jobs were only open to white laborers, and by World War II, the majority of arrabbers were African American.

There aren't many arabbers left, so finding one roaming the streets can be a bit like searching for a needle in a haystack. You can always find them at their stables, though, and they love talking to visitors. You'll see their signature carts and "fancy harnesses," styles that were developed in Baltimore and have always been exclusive to the city. You can visit the stables and pet their horses. They'll even let you sit in their different carts, some of which are for weddings and children's parties, and even a hearse. There have been many controversies surrounding the arabber tradition over the past few years, which is one of the reasons the arabbers are so welcoming and encourage people to come to their stables. The arabber is not an anachronism – they still bring produce to food deserts, servicing some of the poorest neighborhoods, just as their predecessors did. These are men who cherish their animals, respect their history, and love their city.

Address 1102 N Fremont Avenue, Baltimore, MD 21217, +1 (410)385-1277, www.facebook.com/BaltimoreArabbers | **Hours** Unrestricted | **Tip** Sadly much of West Baltimore became a victim of urban decay as people fled to the suburbs. The historic Upton Mansion (811 W Lanvale Street, Baltimore, MD 21217), a stunning 19th-century Greek Revival, is one of those victims. The upside? It's still standing, and it is the perfect specimen to be considered as a legendary haunted house.

9 _ A. T. Jones & Sons
A fashionable flair for the dramatic

Once a thriving strip, Howard Street's block upon block of remarkable art-deco buildings are now abandoned or adorned with "For Rent" signs. When you come to the 700 block, you'll see a storefront that will confuse, and possibly frighten you for a moment if you have coulrophobia. Staring straight at you from the large picture window are the grimacing faces of three large clowns. But this is not a house of horrors. It is A. T. Jones & Sons, a costume company that has been outfitting the nation's finest operatic and theatrical companies since 1868.

Inside, you'll spy rack upon rack of costumes that span centuries of fashion, boxes of props and accessories. You'll meet some of the most talented designers in the business, fabricating patterns, measuring actors, and sewing articles that are nothing short of masterpieces. In the center of the madness, you'll find an elderly gentleman who is one of the more fascinating men in entertainment, owner George Goebel.

Goebel began working at the shop as a teenager back in 1950, when it was still being run by the descendants of A. T. Jones. Costuming was his day job, but his real love was magic. He gradually built a reputation as one of the greatest magicians of his day and then expanded his act to not only include illusions, but daring feats of escape. In 1963, the newly opened Baltimore Convention Center on Pratt Street drew a huge crowd to see Goebel free himself from a straightjacket, while dangling by his feet from a rope affixed to a crane, suspending him 50 feet above the sidewalk below.

In 1972, Goebel purchased the shop from the Jones family, and he is keeping it a family affair. He now runs the shop with his son, who has worked alongside him since he was a child. If you do happen to suffer from coulrophobia, or a fear of clowns, this is the place to face that fear head on.

Address 708 N Howard Street, Baltimore, MD 21201, +1 (410)728-7087 | Hours
Mon–Fri 9am–4pm | Tip The Eubie Blake Cultural Center (847 N Howard Street,
Baltimore, MD 21201, www.eubieblake.org) celebrates the legacy of the local jazz great
with performances, exhibitions, film series, dance workshops, guest speakers, and youth
programming, and community outreach events.

10___The Avenue Bakery
Fresh Poppay's rolls and warm welcomes

After working hard delivering parcels for 30 years, most people would want to put their feet up and enjoy retirement, but Jim Hamlin is most certainly not most people. Growing up in West Baltimore, he saw Pennsylvania Avenue slide into blight and decay – a strip that had once been known as a crown jewel of the African-American community. Jim Hamlin got up and got to work, opening a bakery on the dilapidated strip, defying the naysayers who said that it was a crazy idea that would never work. Over five years later, the Avenue Bakery is thriving and giving people a reason to come back to the neighborhood.

It was enough for Hamlin to feed his community, enough to show that a business could thrive in a place that had been written off. But for a man who has become a community icon, there is no such thing as "enough." He is rightfully proud of the strong traditions and rich history of Baltimore's African-American community, and he's dishing up knowledge alongside his mind-blowing peach cobbler. A television displays local legends Cab Calloway and Billie Holiday on loop. The walls are covered with images and stories of the neighborhood's rich past, as well as images of the historic Royal Theater – one of the most famous stages of the "Chitlin' Circuit" that was crucial to the building of American popular culture. The theater was razed, and Mr. Hamlin is determined to rebuild it, raising money through jazz concerts and other events he stages at the bakery.

As extraordinary a man as Jim Hamlin is, his doors would not have stayed open had he not possessed a special kind of magic: his secret recipe for Poppay's rolls. The inspiration for these delicate, slightly sweet breads came from his mother, but the recipe is 100% Jim. One bite and you'll understand why the Avenue Bakery is something special on every conceivable level. You'll be back soon.

Address 2229 Pennsylvania Avenue, Baltimore, MD 21217, +1 (410)225-3881, www.theavenuebakery.com | **Hours** Wed–Fri 7:30am–2:30pm, Sat 8am–4pm, Sun 10am–2:30pm | **Tip** The Avenue Bakery is a massive booster for the little-known Pennsylvania Avenue Heritage Trail, an underappreciated history walk that explores the history and civil-rights legacy of the area. You can pick up a map at the bakery, and if it isn't too busy, ask Jim's wife up at the counter for some "off the record" stories.

11_Babe Ruth's Orphanage
The Babe as a troubled babe

He's remembered as a New York Yankee, but George Herman "Babe" Ruth was a Baltimore boy. The tiny house in Ridgely's Delight where he was born is worth a look, but his full story requires a visit to the abandoned ruins of the place where he grew up: the orphanage known as St. Mary's Industrial School for Boys.

Six of George's eight siblings died in childhood. His parents worked long hours in a local saloon, which they later owned, neglecting their children in the process. With no parental supervision, coupled with what historians now believe was ADHD, George was a monster of a child. He refused to attend school and instead joined other delinquents running amok in the roughest parts of Baltimore, down on the docks or in the railroad yards, drinking beer, fighting, and chewing tobacco. Unable to control their son, and acknowledging that they could not raise him, his parents forfeited him to the orphanage. He was seven years old.

St. Mary's was a world away from the seedy neighborhood where the Ruth family lived. Run by the Catholic Order of Xaverian Brothers, the orphanage was strict: discipline was enforced, and boys were expected to work hard. All children were given vocational classes, and it was believed that physical activity was essential to build the children's strength. Participation in sports was heavily encouraged, especially baseball.

George became obsessed with the sport, practicing every day and becoming the star pitcher for the orphanage's travelling team. A scout from the Baltimore Orioles heard about him, and when he turned 18, he was legally adopted by the team's talent scout, Jack Dunn. Legend has it that as he attended his first major league practice with Dunn close by, one of his teammates teased him by shouting "Look at Dunnie and his new babe!" The name stuck, and George Herman would be forever known as "Babe" Ruth.

Address 3225 Wilkens Avenue, Baltimore, MD 21229 | Hours Unrestricted, viewable from the outside only | Tip Around the corner from Camden Yards you'll find the Babe Ruth Birthplace Museum (216 Emory Street, Baltimore, MD 21230, www.baberuthmuseum.org), where you'll be able to experience his troubled early days firsthand, as well as view thousands of priceless baseball artifacts.

12 Baltimore Mural Project

Making the city a museum

It's impossible to drive through the streets of Baltimore without noticing art everywhere. Since 1975, the Baltimore Mural Program has committed itself to making every corner of the city more beautiful. Unlike similar programs in other cities, the BMP does not discriminate against neighborhoods, meaning you're as likely to stumble upon surprising pieces of artistic genius in poor neighborhoods as you would in gentrified or tourist-centric areas. The murals become local landmarks ("Take a left at the rainbow horse!"), and they are a tremendous source of pride for the communities. Some murals are abstractions, some winks to local lore, and many are celebrations of the neighborhoods themselves. On the corner of Washington Boulevard and Barre Street, a mural greets you at the gateway to one of Baltimore's most quirky-sounding neighborhoods: Pigtown.

Pigtown sprung up around the railroad, which was invented on the land that now houses the B&O Railroad Museum (a must see in itself!). The Baltimore and Ohio Railroad was one of the most important railways in America, connecting the coastal ports to the Midwest. Goods and passengers would be taken westward. Products would be loaded onto the B&O back to Baltimore to be shipped out of the port and distributed up and down the East Coast. One of the more fantastic of these arrivals? Thousands and thousand of pigs sent from the farms of Middle America. The slaughterhouses were located a few miles away in Federal Hill, so each time a shipment came in, the streets would be cleared, and the pigs were marched down the road. This quirky bit of history is kept in Baltimoreans' memories by a two-story mural depicting a steam locomotive and in the forefront, a group of pink pigs with their leader staring straight at you, as if he could speak the message emblazoned across the header: "Welcome to Historic Pigtown."

Address Corner of Washington Boulevard and W Barre Street, www.baltimorearts.org/
cultural-affairs-2/mural-program | **Hours** Unrestricted | **Tip** There are over 250 city-
sponsored murals that dot the streets of Baltimore, making it a fun scavenger-hunt for
art lovers. Find a map at www.promomotionandarts.org.

13 Baltimore School For The Arts

Tupac Shakur danced Balanchine

One of the greatest rappers of all time, Tupak Shakur was synonymous with the Los Angeles sound of the early 1990s, a poet whose lyrics still strongly resonate today. He was murdered in 1994 as a result of a bitter East Coast/West Coast rap feud – ironic, as Tupac spent the majority of his teenage years in Baltimore.

He moved here when he was 13 years old, living in a small apartment at 3955 Greenmount Avenue. The political consciousness that became a hallmark of his music was heavily influenced by his activist mother, the poverty they both lived in, and the urban decay he witnessed on the city streets. Tupac and his best friend from Roland Park Middle School formed a rap duo, performing wherever they could: rec centers, street corners, and private parties.

Tupac's love of performing inspired him to audition for the elite Baltimore School for the Arts, majoring in theater. He was a voracious reader who spent most of his free periods in the library, devouring plays by Chekhov, Ibsen and Shepard. He claimed than upon graduation, he wanted to pursue a career as a Shakespearean actor because, "You have to be the very best in order to do Shakespeare." He'd put on impromptu performances on the street, rap-battling friends in the Inner Harbor near where he worked, grabbing a role on any stage that would give him a chance. If it wasn't enough to be an actor, musician, and a poet, Tupac was also a gifted dancer. Remarkably, he performed the role of the Mouse King in the school's production of the *Nutcracker* ballet.

Sadly these salad days had to end, and before he was able to graduate, the Shakur family moved out to California, where his mother hoped to find a fresh start. Most of the story his fans know was written in the years that followed, but the preface for the man who became a legend was written in Baltimore.

Address 712 Cathedral Street, Baltimore, MD 21201, +1 (443)642-5165,
www.bsfa.org | **Hours** Viewable from the outside only | **Tip** Tupac got his first taste
of success at the Enoch Pratt Library (1531 W North Avenue, Baltimore, MD 21217,
www.prattlibrary.org), where he won a rap contest about literacy, with lyrics he wrote
about the importance of getting a library card. The lyrics in question now reside in the
special collections department at the library's main branch in Mount Vernon.

14 BAMF Café
Nerd Power!

Attention Whovians, Trekkies, Whedonites, Potterheads and Nerf-herders: you have a "safe space" in Charm City. BAMF Café makes no illusions as to what it is or what they love. They proudly trumpet their nerdom, with rotating window displays that are homages to their passions. It's very hard not to do a double take while driving by – it's not every day you come across a full-sized Dalek in a shop window.

Inside you'll find an early 20th-century soda fountain that's been converted into a fandom paradise. Every wall is covered with pop culture artwork and memorabilia, every surface covered in action figures and statuettes. In the back you'll find one-of-a-kind items from local artists that celebrate their favorite fandoms. The menu, of course, has a pop-culture theme, with sandwiches, salads, and great non-alcoholic drinks that have existed only in our childhood memories, like homemade Ecto-Cooler.

What really makes BAMF one of the most unique places to spend an hour or two isn't the theme, but the community there. No matter the time, there's always something playing on the big screen that will inspire you to chat with the staff and other patrons, like cartoons from the 80s and 90s, or reruns of RuPaul's Drag Race. Special theme days, like X-Men day (the owner's favorite fandom) bring fans in from open to close to watch movies, talk comics, and grab a great cup of coffee (Cyclops Red Eye, anyone?). And we all know it's more fun to watch your favorite shows with people who are as crazy about them as you are. BAMF is the spot where people gather to watch first-run broadcasts of television's most intense series, not only for the thrill of company, but also to have people to dissect entire episodes with as they happen. Truly, this is nerd paradise, and not a single person would feel ashamed of that name. After all, the nerds shall inherit the earth.

Address 1821 N Charles Street, Baltimore, MD 21201, +1 (667)930-3371, www.twitter.com/bamfcafe | **Hours** Mon–Thu 8am–6:30pm, Fri 8am–9pm, Sat 10am–10pm | **Tip** Half a block south is the Lost City Diner (1730 N Charles Street, Baltimore, MD 21201, www.lostcitydiner.com), a retro sci-fi themed space specializing in superlative burgers and classic American comfort foods, much of which is vegetarian or vegan friendly. Make good use of the free jukebox.

15_ Bazaar Baltimore
Come to the dark side

Looking for a taxidermied squirrel? A staged photograph of a well-dressed corpse from the Victorian era? Perhaps a painting created by none other than Charles Manson? You'll find no shortage of the bizarre at Bazaar Baltimore, the place for oddities in the odd neighborhood of Hampden.

Opened on a whim by two friends in 2013, Bazaar has become the destination for those with an eye for the abnormal. The owners scour auctions, antique shows, and flea markets, buying the objects that most traditional antiques dealers find too spooky to keep in their shops. Noted taxidermy artists sell their finest work on commission here. Occasionally, people bring in objects they've found in their attic that they would like to live without, or an item they've discovered hidden amongst the possessions of the recently deceased.

Bazaar not only carries hallmarks of the oddity genre, like antique Ouija boards and animal skulls. You'll also find things so utterly fantastic, it will take you a few minutes to even convince yourself of their existence. Consider the sculptures made out of intestines: who considers intestines to be an artistic medium? What inspires them? Where did the intestines come from in the first place? And perhaps more unnerving than preserved organs and severed animal heads: artwork created by some of America's most notorious serial killers. Over the years, Bazaar has carried many pieces by some of the most prolific ones, particularly John Wayne Gacy, the serial "Killer Clown."

If you can't find something that piques your interest at Bazaar, perhaps you should try your hand at making your own oddity. Workshops have become so popular that the shop now has a dedicated space to hold taxidermy classes and even private workshops for birthdays and other events. Bazaar is a place that can make anything unique by inviting in the extraordinary.

Address 3534 Chestnut Avenue, Baltimore, MD 21211, +1 (410)844-3015, www.bazaarbaltimore.com | Hours Mon & Wed–Sat noon–6pm, Sun noon–5pm | Tip Next door you'll find a beautiful mural that reads "Stay Humble, Baltimore" – a popular photo spot for tourists. But it's not just a backdrop – it's the sign for Stay Humble, considered by many to be the best tattoo shop in town (801 W 36th Street, Baltimore, MD 21211, www.stayhumblebaltimore.com).

16 Bengies Drive-In

Happy days are here again

When the first drive-in movie theater opened in 1933, it became an instant success, and soon the concept was found from coast to coast, becoming a cherished fixture of classic Americana. During its heyday there were more than 5,000 theaters in the United States, but with the growing popularity of television, the advent of the air-conditioned multiplex, and eventually the VCR, they began to close as quickly as they opened. Today it's believed there are fewer than 320 classic theaters still standing. If you've driven yourself into Baltimore, you're in luck! Prepare to party like it's 1959 at Bengies Drive-In Theatre, a nostalgic throwback that's also a state-of-the-art cinematic experience.

People have been pulling their cars up to Bengies since 1956 for double and triple features of the newest Hollywood releases (three movies for the price of one!), as well as classic flicks and special events. Projected on a 52' x 120' screen – supposedly the largest classic movie screen in the US – the films are truly larger than life, which is an absolute must for a gigantic summer blockbuster. After all, they call them movie *theaters* – certainly there should be far more spectacle and flair than sitting at home watching a movie on Netflix!

Just because Bengies is "vintage" doesn't mean it's old fashioned. The projection systems have been upgraded to digital, resulting in crystal clear pictures as vivid as in your local megaplex. They do keep a touch of the old school on hand, retaining a 35mm film projector for screening the classic trailers, movie clips, vintage cartoons and advertisements that run between the features. There is always something up on the screen from the moment the sun sets, while you're stretching your legs between features, chasing after errant children, or grabbing a bag of popcorn, burgers, fries, and drinks from the snack bar, you'll always be entertained. Bring your date or pile the kids into the car for the perfect movie night.

Address 3417 Eastern Boulevard, Middle River, MD 21220, +1(410)687-5627, www.bengies.com | **Hours** Movies start at dusk | **Tip** Nearby off Kaiser Road, you'll find Dundee Natural Environment Area, a swath of land that has been preserved in a completely untouched state. Popular with outdoor enthusiasts, it's particularly well loved for its calm kayaking and paddle-boarding conditions (www.facebook.com/pages/Dundee-Natural-Environment-Area/126698310709299).

17_Betty Cooke Jewelry
Madame of modernism

You can find one of the most influential modernist designers of the 20th century tucked away in Baltimore like a Russian doll. Bypass downtown and the arts districts and instead head north on Falls Road, towards the mundane buildings with a small gatehouse. Follow markers "to the shops," which are also hidden within this hidden place. Pass through a corridor, and at last you arrive in the center of the Village Square at Cross Keys, a planned community that feels refreshingly anachronistic. Walk the perimeter until you find The Store Ltd. and step inside a vestige of the mod 1960s.

You'll be surrounded by goods that would not be out of place in the finest Madison Avenue boutiques. But before you browse the shelves of aesthetically flawless merchandise, make your way to a corner in the back. There is where you'll find the true treasure at the end of your quest: Betty Cooke, living icon of modernist fashion.

A native of Baltimore, Betty attended MICA where, by her senior year, she was making and selling jewelry. The significance of her work is best told by the language (and existence) of a placard that accompanies some of her work at the Museum of Modern Art in New York City: "In the 1940s, she was at the forefront of modern jewelry design, moving away from precious metals and gems to focus on pure form."

Her Bauhaus-influenced pieces can be found at many of the world's most important museums, such as the Costume Institute at the Metropolitan Museum of Art. If that isn't enough to convince you that purchasing one of her pieces is a worthwhile investment, you should know that she has won the De Beers Diamond Today Award – known as "the Oscars of Jewelry" – not once, but twice. Her work is not cheap, but authentic Betty Cookes are not simple accessories – they are true artistic masterpieces that are as relevant today as they were 70 years ago.

Address 24 Village Square, Baltimore, MD 21210, +1 (410)323-2350, www.villageofcrosskeys.com | **Hours** Mon–Sat 10am–6pm, Sun noon–4pm | **Tip** Betty Cooke isn't the only famous jeweler in town – head across the courtyard to visit the storefront of Rebecca Meyers, whose handmade nature-inspired creations are considered must-haves for serious modern jewelry collectors (5100 Falls Road, 14 Village Square, Baltimore, MD 21210, www.rebeccamyersdesign.com).

18 __ Billie Holiday Alley

A child remembered, a life celebrated

Before she became the jazz legend known as "Lady Day," she was Eleanor Fagan, child of misfortune, child of Baltimore.

She was the child of unmarried teenagers: 13-year-old Sadie Fagan and 15-year-old Clarence Holiday, a banjo player who played with many jazz bands of the day. Her father gave her the nickname of Bill because she was a tomboy, and she later changed it to Billie after her favorite movie star, Billie Dove. Clarence went to fight in World War I, after which he chose to follow his musical ambitions instead of returning to his family.

Sadie headed to Philadelphia to find work, leaving Billie with her extended family in East Baltimore. She had a close relationship with her great-grandmother, who peacefully died one night while sleeping in bed with Billie. Billie went into shock and was hospitalized for a month, but there was no sympathy upon her return. Her cousins regularly beat her severely.

A year later, Sadie returned to Baltimore and moved with her daughter to 219 Durham Street. Sadie caught a neighbor trying to rape a then 11-year-old Billie. He was arrested, Sadie moved them down the block to 217 Durham Street. Billie, now 12 and a dropout, began polishing the marble stoops of row houses for pennies and ran errands at a local whorehouse. Her mother once again left to find work, and by 1929, scarred by a town that brought her nothing but pain, Billie joined Sadie in Harlem. The next time she stepped foot in Baltimore, she was a star.

Today, Durham Street is a shrine to its most famous daughter. Large murals of Lady Day are painted on the sides of buildings and depicted in the Baltimore artistic tradition of painted screens, and gardenias painted by school children are found at every turn. The pain in Billie Holiday's voice resonated with millions. So it is fitting that the street that witnessed so much of it could also inspire such beauty.

Address South Durham Street between E Pratt and Gough Streets, Baltimore, MD 21231 | **Hours** Viewable from the outside only | **Tip** Head around the corner to look at the window display of The Antique Man, possibly the most eclectic antiquities broker in the city. If you're in luck, he'll be in the shop on the day of your visit and allow you to browse the wonders inside (1806 Fleet Street, Baltimore, MD 21231, www.theantiquemanltd.com).

19 __ Black History Metro Stations

Riding through the centuries of African American

Art is everywhere in Baltimore. There's even art under your feet: the MTA Metro features 16 iconic permanent art installations, four of which were designed by local artists, and one designed by a man largely considered as one of the most important artists of the 20th century.

Hovering above the platform of the Lexington Market station are long concrete beams that have been transformed by Pat Alexander, a faculty member at MICA. The piece, called *Geometro*, is a ceramic mosaic that is evocative of traditional African textiles, with sharp angular patterns in vivid colors. As you move along this work of art, it continually transforms itself with your change of perspective.

At State Center, kinetic sculptor Paul Daniel suspended his mobile *Ventner* from the ceiling, an abstract whirligig of twisted and forged metal. Another abstract piece can be found at the Rodgers Avenue Station, where a monolith called *Weathering Steel* was installed by Gregory Moring. The series of simple, interlocking shapes is meant to evoke the steel machinery of Baltimore's manufacturing past and was left untreated so that it would be slowly consumed by rust and decay. In the Mondawmin station, you will see three, large colorful faces staring down at you: a backlit photographic and ink montage called *Archetype*, by R. Thomas Gregory.

The most famous of all the pieces is *Uproar* in the Upton Station. This Italian glass mosaic is yet another public memorial to Billie Holiday, depicting her performing with six musicians. Its creator, Romare Bearden, was not from Baltimore, but a member of the Harlem Renaissance in New York City, and eventual recipient of an honorary doctorate from MICA. His many works examining the relationships between members of the African-American community made him one of the most highly regarded artists of the 20th century.

Address Lexington Market Station, State Center Station, Rogers Avenue Station, Mondawmin Metro Station, and Upton Station, www.mta.maryland.gov | Hours Mon–Fri 5am–midnight, Sat & Sun 6am–midnight | Tip Leon's of Balto is one of the oldest loud-and-proud gay bars in America. Opened in 1890, it became gay-friendly after World War II when it was a refuge for artists and beatniks, and it would later become a full fledged gay bar in 1957 (1742 Light Street, Baltimore, MD 21230, www.leonsbaltimore.tripod.com).

20___BUGSS

Mad scientists welcome, and happy ones too

The words "thriving underground science scene" might not be a phrase you ever thought you'd hear, but when you think about it, it makes sense that Baltimore would have one. After all, three of America's best hospitals are located here – Mercy Medical Center, Johns Hopkins, and the University of Maryland Shock Trauma Center – the latter two being extensions of highly competitive and world-renowned medical schools. Biotech companies have begun to flock here thanks to government initiatives and tax breaks. While certainly an affordable city for young scientists, they usually don't have the personal budget for a home laboratory to conduct experiments "for fun." That was the impetus behind the creation of the Baltimore Underground Science Space (BUGSS) in 2012, but its mission, along with its members, has grown into so much more.

When asked to describe the average person at BUGSS, Program Director Dr. Sarah Luhn says it's an impossible task. On any given day you'll find the lab full of artists, engineers, teachers, students, university faculty, professional scientists, and people of all ages who are just beginning a love affair with science. Inquisitive children often come through their doors, as well as retirees who are looking to expand their minds and have new intellectual adventures. Some come to take the first step in developing a product, while some are there to make new friends and "play" with like-minded individuals (note that they are self-proclaimed "nerds," and it is most definitely not a four-letter word here).

A thorough knowledge of science is not a prerequisite for a visit – they warmly (and excitedly!) welcome people who have not much more than curiosity. There are many ways to get involved: free seminars and workshops, volunteering as an assistant, or joining a low-cost class to dive deeper into a specific topic or learn lab skills.

Address 101 N Haven Street, Suite 105, Baltimore, MD 21224, +1 (410)732-0947,
www.bugssonline.org | Hours Tue–Fri & Sat evenings; check website for classes and
events | Tip In summertime, Baltimoreans cool down with snowballs: shaved ice doused
with syrup and toppings. Old-fashioned egg custard with marshmallow whip is one of the
most popular choices, and Icy Delights may make the best one in town (3930 Fleet Street,
Baltimore, MD 21224, www.facebook.com/myicydelights).

21 Carrollton Viaduct

Trainspotting over two centuries

Baltimore was one of the most important railroading cities of the 18th century, with the Baltimore & Ohio (B&O) Railroad leading the way in America's westward expansion and igniting the Industrial Revolution. What's lesser known is that the railroads *started* here. The first tracks were laid in Pigtown on the grounds of what is now the B&O Railroad Museum, a must-visit for railroad enthusiasts. And something even more exciting lies just a few miles away, spanning across Gwynns Falls: the Carrollton Viaduct, the first and oldest (and still active) railroad bridge in the United States.

Ground was broken for the railroad in 1828 by the last living signer of the Declaration of Independence, Charles Carroll. The plan was to run the track through the Patapsco River Valley to Ellicott's Mills, a bustling manufacturing center 13 miles west. The viaduct over the falls is 312 feet (95 meters) long and rises 65 feet (20 meters) from its foundations.

While the route was quite a sight for the passengers, the decision as to where to lay the track did not have the scenery in mind: the bridge over the falls allowed the B&O to travel between hills and mountains, providing a relatively flat and easy grade. Less strain was put on the steam engines hauling heavy rail cars, not to mention less fuel required and faster trips. Higher profits attracted investors to help expand the railroad. Within 50 years, Baltimore had become one of the most important ports in the country and a major transport hub for livestock and coal.

You can purchase train tickets at the B&O museum to take a train ride across the viaduct. Railroad enthusiasts must go see the viaduct from below as well – check train schedules to make sure you catch one going over the bridge. You'll be standing in the shoes of the men who envisioned this modern wonder that changed the nation nearly 200 years ago.

Address Gwynns Falls near Carroll Park, Baltimore, MD 21230 | **Hours** Unrestricted | **Tip** The B&O Railroad Museum tells the fascinating story of the role of the railways in the American Civil War. Walk through the exhibits and then board a train that will take you on the first American railroad line over the Carrollton Viaduct and straight to historic Ellicott City Station – another must for any railfan (901 W Pratt Street, Baltimore, MD 21223, www.borail.org).

22__Chaps Pit Beef

Who needs crabs when you can have BBQ?

When you think Baltimore cuisine, you probably think of crabs. While it's true they are a very big deal, they're too expensive to be an every day (or even every week) meal.

South of the Mason-Dixon line, every state has its own style of barbecue. Baltimore lays just 35 miles below it, putting it in the "gray area" between the North and Dixie. So Baltimoreans don't quite have the technical tradition of slow-smoking meats over a wood fire, but they've certainly got their own style of barbecue.

True barbecue is low and slow, but pit beef is nothing of the sort. It begins with a huge chunk of generously seasoned bottom round, seared on a metal grate over a 500-degree charcoal fire, then moved towards the periphery to continue cooking via indirect heat. The result is moist, tender, and intensely flavored beef that is sliced thin and piled high on a Kaiser roll. "Fixins" can include barbecue sauce, ketchup, and mustard, but to eat pit beef like a real Baltimorean, you want a few slices of raw onion and a thick slathering of a nasal-clearing horseradish concoction affectionately known as "Tiger Sauce."

When a city develops a "signature" dish, you've got a topic locals will passionately argue over. There are many excellent cases made for Pioneer Pit Beef and Jake's Grill, but neither can be considered to be the city's best because, well, neither is technically within the city limits (though if you have a car, they're *highly* recommended as part of an ad hoc pit beef tour). Beef Baron's at the farmers market has been slicing up some of the best beef outside of Texas since 1975, but unless you're in town on a Sunday between April and December, you're completely out of luck. The truth of the matter is there really is no such thing as "the best": all pit beef is good pit beef, and there is not a single item served at Chap's that will make you regret the trip.

Address 5801 Pulaski Highway, Baltimore, MD 21205, +1 (410)483-2379, www.chapspitbeef.com | **Hours** Daily 10:30am–10pm | **Tip** Few thing compliment beef better than an ice-cold beer. Head north to the Oliver Brewing Company (4216 Shannon Drive, Baltimore, MD 21213, www.oliverbrewingco.com), one of Baltimore's first craft-beer brands that has been brewing for over 20 years.

23 _ The Charmery
Scoop, Scoop-ay-oop

Ice cream had always been considered a rare and expensive dessert served only to the wealthy elite, until 1851 when a Baltimore milk dealer named Jacob Fussell developed a way to mass-produce and distribute it. The title "Ice Cream Capital" lasted only about a decade, as Fussell opened plants in New York, Washington, DC, and Boston, making it the hottest (and coldest) dessert in America.

Baltimore could probably have reclaimed the title in 2013 when The Charmery opened its doors and began serving some of the best ice cream on the planet. A true mom and pop operation, David and Laura Iliff Alima fell in love over their shared love of ice cream and dreamed of opening a place of their own. While working at day jobs, they'd use weekends and vacation time to travel the country and visit other ice cream shops, learn the craft, and taste flavors far beyond chocolate and vanilla. A commitment to using the highest quality ingredients from local farm producers, coupled with a gift of seemingly boundless imagination, makes this place unlike any ice cream parlor.

Their signature flavors are now considered true Baltimore classics, such as a version of cookies & cream made with local Berger cookies, and a creamy Tahitian vanilla swirled with a thick ribbon of sweet and salty Old Bay Caramel (an absolute must try). The flavors rotate and change on a whim and include Cheddar Cheese & Ritz Crackers, Buttermilk Cornbread, Mango Sticky Rice, and a concoction of milk and multiple sugary breakfast cereals named "Saturday Morning Cartoons." The small batches make it easy to accommodate inspiration when it strikes.

Free tastes are given at the counter to help you with your decision, though, honestly, no one would blame you for visiting more than one time in a day. Ice cream this good is certainly worth the extra time working it back off at the gym.

Address 801 W 36th Street, Baltimore, MD 21211, +1 (410)814-0493, www.thecharmery.com | **Hours** Sun–Thu noon–10pm, Fri & Sat noon–11pm | **Tip** West 36th Street, aka "The Avenue," is one of the best antiquing destinations in the region, with stores specializing in fashion, vinyl, oddities, home goods, books, artwork, and more. Bring your wallet, but set a budget first (W 36th Street, Baltimore, MD 21211).

24 Chesapeake & Allegheny Live Steamers

Tiny trains, big engineers

There are all sorts of railroad enthusiasts in the world. Railfans have a general interest in the topic, studying this history of railways and engaging in preservation efforts. Trainspotters are like scavenger hunters, traveling near and far, keeping an eye out for different models across the world until they've seen them all. Model engineers build miniatures in highly precise detail. Then there are the "live steamers," men and women who don't just want to build model railways: they want to ride them. And then there's Baltimore's Chesapeake & Allegheny Live Steamers Preservation Society, a club of live steamers that don't just want to ride the models by themselves, but share their passion and enthusiasm with anyone who is willing to come visit them in Leakin Park.

These live steam trains may be tiny, but they generate larger-than-life enthusiasm for the golden age of locomotives. The ten-acre tracksite has over two miles of hand-laid track, self-financed through the club's members. A ⅛" scale train offers free rides to the public on the second Sunday of each month and during special park events. But this is not just some simple amusement park ride. The steamers are faithful replicas of the locomotives and cars of years ago, with complex parts and machinery that run precisely as they did way back when. The boilers are powered by burning coal, the pressure regulated by a system of valves operated by skilled conductors, the wheels turned by pure steam.

The chugging of the engine, the staccato clacking of the wheels on the track – those aren't artificial sound effects. The train conductors explain the ins and outs of the steam locomotives and show you how antique machinery is as much an art form as it is technology. You may just become a live steamer yourself before the end of your visit.

Address 1925 Eagle Drive, Gwynn Oak, MD 21207, +1 (410)448-0730, www.calslivesteam.org | Hours Second Sunday of each month, Apr–Nov 11am–3:30pm | Tip In the middle of Leakin Park stands a vast estate that would make any millionaire jealous – knowing that this was merely a summer home makes it all the more enviable. The Crimea Estate belonged to Thomas Winans, the engineer who built the Russian Railway between Moscow and St. Petersburg, and features a Gothic chapel, honeymoon cottage, carriage house, and an expansive meadow alongside the Italianate stone mansion that is its centerpiece (1901 Eagle Drive, Baltimore, MD 21207, www.friendsoforiandahouse.com).

25 __ Club Charles
Studio 54 for bums and a ghost

Club Charles is a dive bar with celebrity pedigree. It's dimly lit to the point of total darkness, save for the glow of an antique jukebox and neon lights that give it the aura of a waiting room in hell. It was opened as the Wigwam in 1951 by Esther West, the type of larger-than-life character that made Baltimore famous by movie director John Waters, a longtime regular whom you may spot at the bar, dry martini in hand. He and the late, great Divine referred to it as "Studio 54 for bums." It had the distinction of being the scariest bar in all of Baltimore. A 1981 facelift included a name change to Club Charles, but the vibe stayed the same. The sense of danger (alongside the cheap booze) continued to attract the emotionally homeless, freaks, geeks, and creatives. It's no wonder, then, why a ghost would feel at home there and never want to leave.

An employee called Frenchie worked at the Wigwam. His real name was Edouard Neyt. Born outside of Paris, he was a double agent during World War II, spying on the Nazi party. Immigrating to Baltimore postwar, he bounced around town waiting tables, eventually landing at the Wigwam and moving into the apartment upstairs. In 1979 he was found dead in his bedroom from acute alcoholism. Soon after his death, people began spotting a diminutive man walking around in a waiter's uniform who would suddenly disappear. Bottles would be shuffled around; glasses would be found on the bar after it had been closed for the night; an old payphone that did not accept incoming calls suddenly began to ring and would continue even after it was picked up.

One of Frenchie's signature moves when he was alive was to interrupt a regular poker game that ran in the back by messing up people's hair and sitting on their laps. After his passing the interruptions continued, with people feeling phantom fingers running through their hair.

Address 1724 N Charles Street, Baltimore, MD 21201, +1 (410)727-8815, www.clubcharles.us | Hours Daily 6pm–2am | Tip The restored gem that is the Charles Theater (1711 N Charles Street, Baltimore, MD 21201, www.thecharles.com) is now the region's premiere art-house cinema, showing indie films, operas live from the Met in New York, classic movies, and a highly popular Japanese anime series.

26 The Continental Building
Original nesting grounds of the Maltese Falcon

If you're a fan of film noir, crime shows, and mysteries, you've got Dashiell Hammett to thank for that. The undisputed master of the hard-boiled detective novel, Hammett's typewriter gave us the names that would define the genre. The Continental Op. Nick & Nora Charles. Sam Spade. Their gritty street smarts came from from Hammett's life experience. The sleaze and danger came from the seedy underbelly of Baltimore.

Hammett moved to Baltimore when he was six, the son of an alcoholic womanizer who could never hold down a job. When he was 14, Hammett was forced to drop out of school. His first job was as a messenger for the B&O railroad, where he developed a taste for multiple vices. To get off the same path that derailed his father, he left the rail yards to work for the Pinkerton Detective Agency. PI James Wright promoted and trained Hammett and would serve as the inspiration for the Continental Op (and the character's name derived from their office building).

Hammett spent seven years consorting with the people who would make up the world of his stories: petty criminals, crime bosses, corrupt cops and politicians, and the rich men in ivory towers who pulled the strings. Working class stiffs, femmes fatales, hookers with hearts of gold were heroes. His detectives would be his flawed anti-heroes, whose lives were tainted with the vices they used to cope with the horrors they witnessed. There were no white knights in Dashiell Hammett's world – everyone and everything was broken in some way.

The Continental Building, renamed One Calvert Plaza, is an impressive Beaux Arts skyscraper, one of the few buildings that survived the great fire of 1904. When you stand across the street from the main entrance and look up, you can see sculptures of two regal birds that have been said were the inspiration for possibly his greatest story of all: *The Maltese Falcon*.

Address One Calvert Plaza, or 210 E Baltimore Street, Baltimore, MD 21202 | **Hours** Viewable from the outside only | **Tip** Slip into the lobby of the Marriott SpringHill Suites (120 E Redwood Street, Baltimore, MD 21202) around the corner, formerly home to an opulent early 20th-century bank. Down the stairs you'll find the original bank vault, brilliantly repurposed as the hotel's conference room.

27   Davidge Hall

Bring out your dead

The human body was once a total mystery, and the pursuit of medical knowledge was controversial, if not sacrilegious. The University of Maryland broke the barriers and opened the country's first public medical school in 1807. Davidge Hall is the oldest medical teaching facility in America, built in 1811 as a replacement for the original, which was burned down by an angry mob enraged by the science inside. Today the building is used for lectures, but 200 years ago its primary purpose was the dissection and study of cadavers. Using bodies for scientific study was illegal in the 1800s, so for the first 70 years of its existence, the medical school was fueled by stolen corpses.

If you were ill in the early 19th century, you'd visit a barbershop surgeon or a faith healer. It was believed that when people died, their bodies needed to be buried intact, prepared for the resurrection. Cutting one open allowed the person's soul to escape, preventing them from ascending to heaven and condemning them to wander the earth as a ghost for eternity.

Grave robbing was lucrative – $20 per body, $400 in today's terms. Bodies had to be fresh with few signs of decomposition, not just for the purposes of study, but to help the robbers cover their tracks. They observed burials, paying close attention to the positioning of the body. Knowing the corpse's position when they returned later that night, the robbers would dig a hole at the head of the coffin until the box was smashed open. A large meat hook was slipped under the cadaver's chin to yank it out. The hole was quickly filled in, the flowers and mementos returned to their exact positions, and no one was any the wiser.

Snoop around the hall and see if you can find the location of the secret spiral staircases used to deliver stolen corpses clandestinely to one of the secret dissection rooms, now used as the offices of Davidge Hall.

Address 520 W Lombard Street, Baltimore, MD 21201, +1 (410)706-7454, www.medicalalumni.org.davidge-hall | Hours Mon–Fri 8:30am–5pm; register for walking tours on the website | Tip At the University of Maryland School of Nursing, you'll find a Living History Museum dedicated to the profession and displaying hundreds of historic medical items and personal heirlooms, such as wartime letters and photographs from military nurses (655 W Lombard Street, Baltimore, MD 21201, www.nursing.umaryland.edu/about/community/museum).

28_Detective Comics #27

Dark Knight meets world

It's not true that Geppi's Entertainment Museum is the greatest museum in the world (the Louvre would probably disagree), and it's even hard to claim as the best in a city full of countless exceptional ones. But as museums go, none will make you smile as wide as Geppi's. You may even lose control and act a bit like a child, which is perfectly understandable, as this is a museum that is devoted to *your* childhood, no matter your age. The founder himself is a man who made a fortune by promising to never grow up.

Steven Geppi began his career as an accidental comic book salesman – by profession he was a mailman – but then his wife grew tired of his growing collection of comics and vintage toys and requested that he get rid of them. In time, however, people began bringing him their own comics to sell, which evolved into a full-time distribution business: Diamond Comic Distribution, which is now the only comic book distribution company in the world. The amount of memorabilia Mr. Geppi has amassed with his considerable wealth is so utterly fantastic that it needed its own museum: 16,000 square feet of nostalgia in the old Camden Yards Railroad Station.

You'll travel the decades room by room and discover toys and relics you've only read about in books: the first ever teddy bear, the original sketches for *Snow White & the Seven Dwarves*, a Howdy Doody doll, priceless Star Wars action figures. But there are two items even more exciting than these – the twin holy grails of pop culture, which are both so rare that they are each worth millions of dollars. You'll find them at the entrance of the comic book room in a glass case all their own: mint condition copies of Detective Comics 27, which introduced the world to Batman, and Action Comics 1, the first ever Superman comic book. Don't worry if you audibly squeal with delight – it's a very common reaction.

Address 301 W Camden Street, Baltimore, MD 21201, +1 (410)625-7060, www.geppismuseum.com | **Hours** Tue – Sun 10am – 6pm | **Tip** The conversion of the historic Camden Yards Train Station (333 W Camden Street, Baltimore, MD 21201, www.baltimore.orioles.mlb.com) into a thriving entertainment area is a major point of pride for the city. If it's baseball season, seeing an Orioles game is a must. Even better: take a behind-the-scenes tour, which can be booked through the team's website.

29 Dickeyville

Little house in the big city

With 140 historic homes, a clapboard church, two roads, and three tiny lanes, Dickeyville is an unlikely urban oasis to find in Baltimore, let alone in the 21st century.

The charming village was founded on the banks of the Gwynns Falls, a 25-mile-long stream that powered nearly all the city's early factories, which in turn made Baltimore a national center of manufacturing and trade. Dickeyville's mills produced flour, paper, and textiles, which were sold up and down the East coast. The town expanded slowly in the early 18th century as demand for its products grew, and the mill owners began building stone houses for their workers, as well as a church and school. In 1871, most of the town, including three mills and the majority of the houses, was sold to Irish immigrant William J. Dickey, who ushered the town into an even greater age of prosperity. The mills now focused on textile production, with the Baltimore & Ohio railroad distributing their goods throughout the country.

As the mills became obsolete and the stock market crashed in 1929, Dickeyville's future was uncertain. But in 1934, two brilliant developers bought the entire town, and went to work restoring it. Any structure that remained structurally sound was preserved, and while the insides would be modernized, the traditional aesthetic of the community would be unchanged. In 1972, the Dickeyville community was listed on the National Register of Historic Places. Today it remains a community of private residents, all of whom are committed to preserving their adopted home. Gardens are meticulously planted; homes are decorated with period touches. You'll very often find friendly people walking the paths or sitting on their porches, happy to have a little chat about anything and everything. And of course, you can always drop by for church services on Sunday. Dickeyville would love to have you.

Address Near the intersection of Interstates 70 and 695, Dickeyville, MD 21207, www.dickeyville.org | Hours Unrestricted | Tip It may seem retro, but roller disco is as big in Baltimore as it was back in the 70s. Many locals say they were wearing skates as soon as they could walk. There's always a good time to be had at Hot Skates, a family-friendly rink that's known as "The Hottest Kid's Party in Baltimore" (1716 Whitehead Road, Woodlawn, MD 21207, www.unitedskates.com/public/woodlawn/index.cfm).

30 Dorothy Parker's Ashes
Excuse my dust

If Dorothy Parker is associated with any place, it's New York City. A critic, satirist and poet, she was a founder of the famous Algonquin Round Table, a daily salon of some of the most prominent and influential writers of the early 20th century. A Jewish girl from Manhattan, she married a stockbroker, wrote for *Vanity Fair*, *Vogue* magazine, and *The New Yorker*. So how is it that her ashes came to be buried in Baltimore?

In a time of segregation and rampant social injustice, Parker was an outspoken critic of hatred and bigotry long before is was an acceptable position for most white Americans. In one of the few trips she made to Baltimore, she met with the equally famous writer and hometown hero H. L. Mencken, who caused her great offense when he began making derogatory remarks about African Americans. She became an outspoken voice for social justice in the 1930s, eventually ending up on Hollywood's blacklist, and had 1,000-page FBI file during the McCarthy era. A great admirer of Dr. Martin Luther King, whom she had never met, she named him the beneficiary of her estate. A year after her death in 1967, Dr. King was assassinated, and her estate was passed to her second listed beneficiary – the NAACP. Her estate was extremely lucrative, as it included the rights and residuals to her entire literary catalog. A less popular part of her estate was her ashes. Unclaimed from the crematorium, they were mailed to her lawyer six years after her death, who placed them in a filing cabinet and charged the estate a "storage fee" for fifteen years. When a biographer discovered them, the NAACP claimed the ashes and brought them to their national headquarters in Baltimore.

In 1988, 21 years after her death, Dorothy Parker was buried in Baltimore, in a circular memorial designed to recall the Round Table. Her epitaph reads exactly as she had requested: "Excuse My Dust."

HERE LIE THE ASHES OF DOROTHY PARKER
(1893 - 1967)
HUMORIST, WRITER, CRITIC,
DEFENDER OF HUMAN AND CIVIL RIGHTS.
FOR HER EPITAPH SHE SUGGESTED
"EXCUSE MY DUST".
THIS MEMORIAL GARDEN IS DEDICATED TO HER NOBLE
SPIRIT WHICH CELEBRATED THE ONENESS OF HUMANKIND,
AND TO THE BONDS OF EVERLASTING FRIENDSHIP BETWEEN
BLACK AND JEWISH PEOPLE.
DEDICATED BY
THE NATIONAL ASSOCIATION FOR THE ADVANCEMENT
OF COLORED PEOPLE
OCTOBER 20, 1988

Dr. William J. Gibson
Chairman, NAACP Board

Dr. Benjamin L. Hooks
Executive Director

Enolia P. McMillan
President

Address 4805 Mount Hope Drive, Baltimore, MD 21215, +1 (410)580-5777,
www.naacp.org | Hours Unrestricted | Tip As long as you're there, you should take
the opportunity to visit the NAACP national headquarters at the same address.
Tours are available, and be sure to set aside time to visit their remarkable library.

31_Dovecote Café

A warm cup of good karma

What separates Dovecote Café from other cafés is an unquantifiable "x-factor" that leaves an indelible mark on every single patron. In their own words, they are "community first, café second." Sometimes spending a morning at Dovecote is more spiritually nourishing then going to church.

It's located in Reservoir Hill, a neighborhood that sidles up against beautiful Druid Hill Park, filled with beautiful – often neglected – townhouses that only hints to its once affluent past. But Dovecote is not on a loud commercial strip, but inexplicably nestled into the middle of a block where an ancient pharmacy once stood. Around it, you can see a neighborhood that is coming back to life: homes restored to their previous glory, flowerbeds planted and blooming, friendly smiles from every person on the street.

While this transformation is the work of many, inside Dovecote you understand what the dictionary definition of community should be, and what the spiritual center of a neighborhood looks like. It is good karma that can't be contained within its four walls, infecting and empowering every person who passes through. At the tables you'll find poets and artists, chefs and farmers, educators and activists, clergy and councilmen. There are no boundaries around anyone, because the energy of the place makes it impossible for you to put them up around yourself. This is a place where friends are made, help is offered, love is shared, and magic is generated.

In a city full of remarkable dining, Dovecote Café is likely the most important eatery in all of Baltimore, for reasons that transcend the written word. It is a place that envelops you snugly like a well-worn robe, a place that will fill you with joy just by virtue of existing. In a perfect world, every city would have a place like Dovecote Café. In Baltimore, we know we're damn lucky that it belongs to us. You will find inspiration at Dovecoat – you may just inspire somebody else.

Address 2501 Madison Avenue, Suite 1F, Baltimore, MD 21217, +1 (443)961-8677, www.dovecotecafe.com | **Hours** Mon–Wed 7am–4pm, Thu & Fri 7am–7pm, Sat 8am–7pm, Sun 8am–4pm | **Tip** Everyone's Place African Cultural Center (1356 W North Avenue, Baltimore, MD 21217) has been a community institution for over 30 years by doing everything the right way: greeting people with open arms and a generous spirit. The mom & pop vibe makes this more than a store, but truly a place to learn about and fully embrace the beauty of African culture.

32 — The Druid &
The Green Man
Chainsaws and ancient tree spirits

The Druids were ancient priests of Celtic Isles, whose existence is shrouded in mystery. Some say they had magical powers. Some say they could communicate with nature. But just about everyone can agree they probably never visited Baltimore. The park that bears their name was inspired not by an ancient visitation, but given by Scottish immigrants who knew the Druids considered the land's oak trees to be sacred. And two hundred years later, the Druids finally arrived.

In 2011, a man named Mark Acton – printing company salesman by day, chainsaw virtuoso by night – was chosen by the city to do something with two red oak stumps. Unlike most artists whose works dot the Baltimore landscape, Acton was not a trained sculptor. Six years prior, he was planning a backyard luau, and he was dismayed by the cost of tiki sculptures. As one would logically conclude in a situation such as that, Acton decided his money would be better spent buying a chainsaw and attempting a DIY version.

Using his skills as an amateur cartoonist, Acton turned a free chunk of discarded wood into a tiki masterpiece, and he was soon getting requests from friends and local businesses for custom sculptures. After honing his skills on 350 more carvings, he was ready to tackle the greatest commission of his career. Each massive stump was twelve feet high and twenty feet around. He worked weekends, cutting large sections away with chainsaws and creating intricate details with hand tools. Crowds gathered to watch the giant faces emerge.

Perhaps it was nothing more than a happy act of insanity that turned Mark Acton into a brilliant woodcarver. But perhaps he was, in fact, called forth by the Druids, who had spent centuries laying in wait in their sacred oak trees, revealing themselves only upon the arrival of the chosen hero, the man who carries a magical chainsaw.

Address 900 Druid Park Lake Drive, Baltimore, MD 21217, +1 (410)396-7900, www.druidhillpark.org | Hours Daily dusk–dawn | Tip The Goya Contemporary Gallery (3000 Chestnut Avenue, Mill Centre, Suite 214, Baltimore, MD 21211, www.goyacontemporary.com) has won international acclaim for its exhibitions, and it's fostering the work of some of the most brilliant artists of our time, like Deborah Kass and Joyce J. Scott, and publishes fine art books through their Goya Girl Press imprint.

33_First Gas Street Lamp
Let there be light

Public illumination was managed for centuries by a "lamplighter," hired to go from post to post, lighting and replacing candles manually, and later, oil lamps. In the early 1800s, a small municipal gas lamp system was unveiled in London. A very clever American took note and determined that Baltimore should be the city that led the country out of proverbial darkness. Remarkably this man was not a robber baron or titan of industry, but rather an artist, Rembrandt Peale.

Peale came from a family of famous portraitists and was the master behind one of the most famous portraits of George Washington, the *Patriae Pater*. Inspired by his father, a painter himself and amateur archeologist who founded the American Museum of Philadelphia, Peale set his sights on Baltimore to create his legacy. He opened the three-story Peale Museum downtown, exhibiting artwork, taxidermy, and specimens of natural history – most notably the complete skeleton of a prehistoric mastodon. While that alone seems quite fantastic, the real draw was the indoor gas lighting. In fact, it was such an extraordinary invention that people would pay a separate admission fee just to see the lamps in use. The frenzy Peale was able to create helped attract investors, and less than a year later, Peale's Gas Light Company of Baltimore unveiled the first public gas street lamp on the corner of North Holiday and East Baltimore Street. In the following decades, the company would lay gas lines to light up the homes of the wealthy, big businesses, and miles of sidewalks, setting the precedent for every other big city.

The gas lamps of Baltimore disappeared when electricity became the standard, but the city never lets its past be easily forgotten. In 1997, an exact replica of Peale's streetlight was erected where it once stood, a quiet reminder to the importance of simple things we often take for granted.

Address Corner of North Holiday Street & East Baltimore Street | **Hours** Unrestricted | **Tip** A short walk away, you'll find the original Peale Museum itself at 225 Holiday Street, the very place the gas light spectacle occurred. It is now vacant and used sporadically for contemporary art shows, though you can still view its contents (including the mastadon) across town at the Maryland Historical Society (201 W Monument Street, Baltimore, MD 21201, www.MHDS.org).

34 First Portable Drill

Checkout the pharmacy

If you're a person for whom the average tourist trap will just not do, the Baltimore Museum of Industry (BMI) is tailor-made for you. It is a celebration of things that make modern life possible but that we take for granted: drinking straws, bottle caps, and umbrellas. While that on the surface may not seem enthralling, the BMI is actually one of the most fun museums you'll ever visit. Travel through time and roam through detailed recreations of shops and factories – like a 1920s newsroom or a 19th-century cannery – built top to bottom with salvaged materials and fixtures. Occasionally you'll find some of the old machinery brought back to life so kids of all ages have the chance to play on it. You'll also spot a familiar Baltimore invention that changed the world: the first practical portable electric drill.

It was 1906 when two 23-year-old gentlemen named Duncan Black and Alonzo Decker became fast friends while working at the local telegraph company. Both born inventors, they began a partnership in their spare time, and with ambition and dreams to spare, sold off their prized possessions to open their own machinery studio in 1910. To keep the bills paid and their experiments funded, they solicited projects from larger companies. While working on a project for the Colt Arms Company, they had a thought: what if they took the grip and trigger from a gun and applied it to a drill? Early mechanical drills were cumbersome and hard to use devices, not to mention expensive. By altering the design and making them portable, soon they were used by a wide array of industries and changed the way things – like houses, appliances, and automobiles – could be built. That initial design became the standard for most electric power tools, from drills to dustbusters (another Black & Decker invention). Still headquartered in the Baltimore region, their legacy continues today.

B&D

THE BLACK & DECKER MFG CO. BALTIMORE. MD. U.S.A.

THE BLACK & DECKER MFG. CO. BALTIMORE MD USA

World's First
Portable Electric Drill

Portable
Electric Drill

BLACK & DECKER Portable Electric Drill

Address 1415 Key Highway E, Baltimore, MD 21230, +1 (410)727-4808, www.thebmi.org |
Hours Tue–Sun 10am–4pm | **Tip** After New York City, Baltimore was the largest port
for immigrants entering the United States. A small Christian boarding house that once
received and housed them has been converted into the Locust Point Immigrant Museum
(1308 Beason Street, Baltimore, MD 21230, www.immigrationbaltimore.org).

35 _ Fluid Movement
Eat your heart out, Esther Williams

For a city where weird is the norm, it takes a lot of effort for something to be considered so insanely beautiful that it borders on mind-boggling. Fluid Movement falls into this category: a community theater that produces original works, casting average people from all walks of life. The twist? It is performed in a public pool through the medium synchronized swimming.

Fluid Movement began nearly twenty years ago in a predictably artsy-fartsy way: a performance artist named Trixie Burneston gathered her colleagues to help stage an aquatic piece she had written. The community response to such a bizarre event was ecstatic, convincing the performers to band together as a troupe to continue producing shows in untraditional form. They immediately wrote a show about local hero and common theatrical inspiration Edgar Allan Poe, done entirely on roller skates. As audiences grew, Fluid Movement kept producing original works, such as *1001 Freudian Nights: A Biography in Bellydance*, and *Star-Spangled Swimmer: A War of 1812 Water Ballet*. A city of weirdos had another flower in its hat.

The first question anyone (logically) asks: how on earth do they find enough people who casually know how to synchronize swim? The answer: they grow their own talent. Free classes every week at a local pool attract anyone who has ever dreamed of trying synchronized swimming. Many of the weekly participants end up joining the troupe. Since they write all their own material, choreography is written to highlight all skill levels and celebrate the talents of all the men and women who make Fluid Movement magical.

If you're in town, swing by Callowhill Aquatic Center at 6pm any Tuesday to try your hand at playing Esther Williams. It is worthwhile to plan a visit to Baltimore directly around Fluid Movement's performance dates – it's an experience like none other you will ever see.

Address 210 Hawthorn Road, Baltimore, MD 21210, www.fluidmovement.org |
Hours Check website for show times. | Tip Need a jolt of caffeine? Check out
High Grounds Coffee Roasters (3201 Eastern Avenue, Baltimore, MD 21224,
www.highgroundscoffee.com), which roasts its beans onsite. You won't just get a great
cup of joe, you'll also be doing some good: High Grounds opened with the mission of
using their sales to help build 100 orphanages throughout the world.

36__Fort McHenry Hospital No. 2

Treating the brave of WWI

Sitting on the tip of the Locust Point peninsula, Fort McHenry was the site of a major battle in the War of 1812, where an unlikely victory for the United States inspired Baltimorean Francis Scott Key to pen The Star Spangled Banner. But during World War I, the grounds were home to the U.S. Army General Hospital No. 2, the largest military hospital in America. One hundred buildings covered nearly every foot of the parks 40-plus acres. Today, one remains.

It began as a receiving hospital for returning servicemen. New weapons of war were inflicting new kinds of injuries. Mustard and chlorine gas burned large swaths of the body and blistered the lungs and throat. Barbed wire gashed and scarred flesh. Soldiers were maimed by tank explosions and long-range machine guns. Out of necessity, Fort McHenry began to transform into a surgical center that revolutionized medicine.

The science of surgery was still relatively new with high mortality rates. In the urgency of wartime this was not an option, and monumental medical discoveries were made at rapid pace in this hospital. Tremendous strides were made in the fields of neurology and neurosurgery; the science of orthopedics took off with the creation of the earliest artificial joints; soldiers who had been permanently disfigured returned home with new facial features thanks to plastic surgery. The concept of occupational therapy was also advanced here, physically rehabilitating fragile patients post-treatment, and teaching them in skills in the first major American effort to train disabled veterans for a postwar life.

The hospital and fort were decommissioned in 1923, with nearly all evidence of its past demolished save the fort and a single hospital building, the former now a famed tourist destination, and the latter an inconspicuous structure used for storage, its history all but forgotten.

Address 2400 E Fort Avenue, Baltimore, MD 21230, +1 (410)962-4290, www.nps.gov/fomc | Hours Daily 10am–5pm | Tip Though they're not an everyday splurge, crabs are most certainly an important part of the Baltimore cuisine, and no one makes them better than LP Steamers (1100 E Fort Avenue, Baltimore, MD 21230, www.locustpointsteamers.com) where they serve hot steamed crabs by the pound alongside pitchers of Natty Boh beer.

37___The Foundery

Dream, design, build

Perhaps you've always wanted to try your hand at making stuff with modern machinery, but didn't think it was possible for you to take up welding or laser engraving recreationally. Not only is it possible, but you could be doing these sorts of things right now if you were to head over to The Foundery. Who can resist the opportunity to use a blowtorch?

Inside The Foundery, you'll use lathes, 3D printers, sandblasters, bandsaws, and many more exciting tools. This is a creation space, where artists, craftsmen, and hobbyists can work and have access to equipment that doesn't exactly fit in a toolshed. And luckily, you can take classes from experts here. Think of it as a badass arts and crafts club. Many classes require absolutely no prior experience, so there's no reason not to jump in and learn something new. There are knife-making workshops, which will show you how to grind metal and properly sharpen your brand new custom blade.

Try your hand at the lost art of bowl turning, where you'll learn to transform a stump of wood into a conversation piece. If you've ever been fascinated by old-time blacksmithing, this is the place that will finally give you the opportunity to put some red-hot metal on an anvil and pound away at it with a hammer. And if you're the klutzy type who thinks all of those activities (despite the intense safety protocols) could result in lost limbs, there are also classes in knitting and sewing.

No matter what you choose to try your hand at, you'll walk out of The Foundery with a piece that you made with your own two hands, and that's better than any generic souvenir. Maybe you'll love it so much, you'll finally be motivated to clean out that toolshed so you can put an anvil in there. If that plan doesn't pan out, The Foundery offers memberships, so you can come in whenever you've got an unshakable urge to do some smithing.

Address 101 W Dickman Street, Baltimore, MD 21230, +1 (855)936-2537,
www.foundery.com | **Hours** Mon 2pm–8pm, Tue–Fri 10am–10pm,
Sat & Sun 10am–4pm | **Tip** One of Baltimore's most beautiful views is in the city's
oldest park, one that flies a bit under-the-radar thanks to its peninsula location.
Riverside Park has everything you need for a great day of recreation: athletic fields,
a picnic pavilion, and a large public swimming pool (301 E Randall Street, Baltimore,
MD 21230, www.baltimore.org/info/leonc-riverside-park).

38_Frederick Douglass Houses

He did do great things in Baltimore

You will find the imprint of the heroic American abolitionist Frederick Douglass all over Baltimore, from the row house he built in Seton Hill to the towering English Elm in Sharp-Leadenhall that shaded him during one of his famous speeches. He spent many years here both as a slave and as a free man, first arriving at the age of 8 to act as a caretaker to the toddler son of Hugh Auld. They lived on Happy Alley, in what he described as "a spare, narrow house" at S Durham Street off Aliceanna Street, and it was there that Auld's wife Sophia began teaching Douglass to read and write until Hugh found out and forbade it. Douglass became literate on his own. By age 12, he was able to read *The Columbian Orator*, which taught him about freedom and human rights. He then joined the Sharp Street Church (see ch. 90).

He left Baltimore when his legal owner, Auld's brother-in-law, made him work in a field where he was constantly beaten. He plotted to escape, but his plans were discovered, and he was sent to prison. When released, he was sent back to Hugh Auld, now living on Philpot Street in Fell's Point, who sent him to work in the shipyards. He became so adept as a caulker it that he became the highest paid man in the yard. Auld allowed him to keep some of his wages, unaware that Douglass was saving up to begin a new life as a freeman. In 1938, with documents borrowed from a sailor, Douglass escaped via the Underground Railroad and headed to New Bedford, Massachusetts, where he married and settled.

Both houses still exist today. The waterfront on which Douglass was once enslaved is now the Frederick Douglass-Isaac Meyers Maritime Park & Museum, home to the Living Classrooms Foundation that provides hands-on learning experience to students from diverse backgrounds and economic classes.

Address Aliceanna Street at S Durham Street, Baltimore, MD 21231 and Philpot Street, Baltimore, MD 21231 | Hours Viewable from the outside only | Tip While Douglass' story is certainly remarkable enough, it gets an additional detail with Douglass Place (1417 Thames Street, Baltimore, MD 21231, www.douglasplace.com). Many years after he escaped from Baltimore, he returned to the city to build a series of row houses in the neighborhood where he was once enslaved, renting them out to now-free African Americans.

39___The Fudgery

Where four local teens became R&B legends

It may seem like nothing more than the ubiquitous candy store that anchors so many touristy destinations, but the Baltimore location of this chain has left an indelible mark on American history. Without The Fudgery, we would not have legendary 90s music group, Dru Hill. Without Dru Hill's success, we wouldn't have Sisqo. And, without Sisqo, we would not have the musical masterpiece that defined the 20th century: The Thong Song.

In 1992, Reservoir Hill teenager Tamir "Nokio" Ruffin decided to pursue a career in music, recruiting four acquaintances Mark "Sisqo the Dragon" Andrews and James "Woody Rock" Green to form an R&B group called 14K Harmony. To gain experience performing in front of crowds, all five got jobs at The Fudgery, where employees are required to sing and dance while working. Rehearsing nearly full-time while slinging fudge, the group quickly coalesced and began winning talent shows across Baltimore.

After two original members quit the group, Larry "Jazz" Anderson, an opera student from Frederick Douglass High School (Cab Calloway's alma mater), was asked to replace them, with the provision that he also become a Fudgery employee. Soon after, the quartet was discovered by the president of Island Black Music, who suggested a name change. In a nod to their Baltimore roots, they renamed themselves Dru Hill, after the iconic grounds adjacent to their childhood homes: Druid Hill Park.

Their self-titled debut album was released in 1996 and achieved platinum status. Their second album, 1998's Enter the Dru, was an even bigger hit, hitting #2 on the Billboard charts and going double platinum. Two years later, Sisqo recorded an independent side project, featuring the insta-classic Thong Song, which led to the group disbanding. Today they reunite periodically to tour and release new music. Not bad for a few teenagers working a fudge counter!

Address 301 Light Street, Baltimore, MD 21202, +1 (410)539-5260, www.fudgeryfudge.com | **Hours** Mon–Sat 10am–9pm, Sun noon–6pm | **Tip** For some free summer fun in the hot, hot sun, visit the Walter Sondheim Fountain (401 Light Street, Baltimore, MD 21202, www.baltimorewaterfront.com/west-shore-park) on the west side of the harbor. It's the most popular (and most fun) splash pad in the city, with kids and adults alike running through getting soaking wet.

40 __ G&A Restaurant
Fine diving

G&A Restaurant, a small greasy spoon in Highlandtown, announces itself to passersby on Eastern Avenue with a big orange sign declaring itself, "The Home of Baltimore's Best Coney Island Hot Dogs." Oddly, the restaurant has nothing to do with the famous Coney Island in New York City. It was founded in 1927 by Greek immigrants Gregory and Alex Diacumacos. In fact, the "Coney Island Specialties" served don't seem to have any ties to true Coney cuisine, and are, in fact, uniquely Baltimore.

Andy Farantos, grandson of the original owners, is the man you'll find behind the counter most days. He knows that the reason that G&A has stayed open for nearly 100 years isn't because of luck or customer's sense of nostalgia – it's because they consistently churn out some of the best blue-collar grub in town. Here you'll find everything to be just about the same way it was on opening day. Even when Andy adds new food items to the menu (like the ethereally paper-thin fried pickles), he makes them exactly the way he pictures his grandfather would have done it. The sliders are a work of art from a different generation – fans of the style served by the legendary "Great White's" (Castle / Manna / Diamond) will find their spiritual home at the Formica counter.

Many joints see the fries as an afterthought, but G&A cuts them by hand and fries them to the peak of golden perfection so that they're sure to make a showing on your personal "best of all time" list. And, if you think you're strong enough to handle it, order yourself a Ravenator burger and hide in a booth where no one can see you: eating 10 ounces of freshly seared beef topped with bacon, shoe-string onions, mushrooms, cheddar, and Andy's secret sauce is an all-in sort of ecstasy that you should be allowed to experience in privacy, away from judgmental eyes that would rather stick to a salad.

Address 3802 Eastern Avenue, Baltimore, MD 21224, +1 (410)276-9422, www.gandarestaurant.com | **Hours** Mon–Sat 7:30am–7pm | **Tip** Across the street is the Markets at Highlandtown (3801 Eastern Avenue, Baltimore, MD 21224), a drab beige storefront that looks to be an unremarkable supermarket. Once you step inside, however, you'll find yourself in an international culinary paradise, with specialty foods from countries such as India, Mexico, Egypt, Korea, and beyond.

41___George Washington's Teeth

Open wide, Mr. President

Overcoming any apprehensions you may have about visiting the dentist will most definitely be worth it, as the National Museum of Dentistry is filled with countless items and stories, like Queen Victoria's personal gold-plated dental instruments. The "crown" jewel of the collection (pun intended), though, is an item of American legend: the false teeth of the first President of the United States, George Washington.

Popular myth claims Washington's teeth were made of wood, and though it makes for a fun schoolyard story, it is unequivocally false. But like in many myths, there is a shred of truth in it. George Washington did wear dentures because of his positively ghastly teeth.

Washington lost his first tooth at the age of 22, and was plagued with serious dental issues throughout his life: decay, pain, nerve damage, and tooth loss. By the time he became president at the age of 57, he had only one tooth remaining – a lone molar in the back of his mouth.

Washington had several sets of dentures made for him, but not a single one was made from wood. The first set was made from actual human teeth, likely from the slaves he had purchased for his Mount Vernon estate. Later he had sets made from ivory taken from hippopotamus and elephant tusks and held together with tightly wound gold springs, which applied constant pressure to his gums to keep the dentures in place. The force his jaw needed to apply constantly in order keep his mouth shut caused excruciating pain, which he treated with a daily dose of laudanum, a legal solution containing opium.

Washington's dentures now rest in a place he would have welcomed in his lifetime. Forty-one years after his death, the University of Maryland School of Dentistry opened its doors in 1840 – the first such institution in the world – eventually putting an end to the days of barbershop tooth extractions, quackery, and pain.

Address 31 S Greene Street, Baltimore, MD 21201, +1 (410)706-0600,
www.dental.umaryland.edu/museum/index.html | Hours Mon–Fri 10am–4pm | Tip The
EMP Collective is a group of young artists that "joined forces to make art and save lives."
Dedicated to creating provocative, multidisciplinary exhibitions, their multi-use arts space
was heralded by *Baltimore* magazine as "one of the boldest visions to change Baltimore"
(307 W Baltimore Street, Baltimore, MD 21201, www.empcollective.org).

42 Giraffe House
Terrifically tall tenants

Every animal at the zoo is special in its own way, but there are some that elicit more excitement than others. We're talking the big ticket, top-billing sorts of species: crazy chimpanzees, stately lions, imposing elephants. The Maryland Zoo has all of those, as well as another top-notch draw that seems to have a little something extra: the majestic Giraffe House.

Fortunately preserved by sheer luck during the zoo renovations (they ran out of money to construct an entirely new one and could only afford interior improvements), the Giraffe House is a mid-century masterpiece. The flying-saucer-shaped building looks as if it belongs in Tomorrowland, with floor to ceiling paned windows, textured exterior panels, and curved steel accents. A central column has been refurbished into a modernist tree of life, integrating into the original wooden starburst ceiling that glows from the building's skylights. You could be forgiven if you didn't notice the giraffes at all.

While they do love their drop-dead gorgeous house, the giraffes seem to enjoy spending most of their time outside where they can wander around under the bright sun and get a little face time with their human guests. The zoo surrounded the area with raised viewing platforms not just for you to be able to get a better selfie with these gentle giants, but also to indulge in a highly affordable once in a lifetime experience: for less money than a cup of coffee, you'll be given a group of acacia leaves that the giraffes will eat right out of the palm of your hand.

2017 brought a very special addition to the menagerie at the zoo: a baby! Willow is the first giraffe to be born at the zoo in over twenty years. This beautiful girl weighed 125 pounds at birth and stood 6 feet tall. Though that's pretty big, it will still be years before she's as big as the rest of her zoo family, who are as tall as twenty feet.

Address 1 Safari Place, Baltimore, MD 21217, www.marylandzoo.org | Hours Daily 10am–4pm | Tip It's impossible to not be impressed by the Victorian-era Palm House at the Rawlings Memorial Botanic Garden, which has been filled with towering trees and exotic blooms since 1888 (3100 Swann Drive, Baltimore, MD 21217, www.rawlingsconservatory.org/virtual-tour).

43_ G. Krug & Sons
Forging through the centuries

It's not easy to stay in business for over 200 years: you need a magical combination of unparalleled skill and phenomenal business sense. Even harder? Staying open for over 200 years in an industry that's been considered completely obsolete for decades. G. Krug & Son have long since departed this earth, yet their little blacksmithing shop on Saratoga Street keeps on churning out artistic wrought ironwork made with little more than fire, hammer, anvil, and a skilled set of hands. Not only is it one of the oldest businesses in Baltimore, it's the oldest blacksmithing shop in all of America.

German immigrant Augustus Schwatka brought his Old World designs and techniques to the New World in 1810 and specialized in small items like nails and hinges. In 1850 Gustav Krug arrived from Germany as well and joined the little shop. His skills soon made him a partner, and they went from crafting household bell hangers to forging the gigantic church bells heard throughout town; from fashioning door hinges to smithing giant wrought-iron doors and gates that flanked Baltimore's most stately buildings.

The works of the past 160 years are visible nearly everywhere in Baltimore and Washington, DC, from the gates of Greenmount Cemetery, to the railings of the Peabody Library and the hospital gates at Johns Hopkins University to the historic buildings of Colonial Williamsburg in Virginia. It's said that there is not a single building in the entire city that does not contain something that has been forged at G. Krug & Sons, even if it's just a single nail.

They're as active today as they were 200 years ago under the watchful eye of Peter Krug, Gustav's great-great-grandson. In 2014, the oldest blacksmith in America also became the first museum dedicated to the craft where you can see not just antiques, but also watch the newest generation of blacksmiths working on machinery that is well over a century old.

Address 415 W Saratoga Street, Baltimore, MD 21201, +1 (410)752-3166, www.gkrugandson.com | **Hours** Mon–Fri 7am–3:30pm | **Tip** One of the most beautiful edifices can be found on the corner of Franklin and Eutaw Streets. Charles Fish & Son is a long forgotten furniture shop, but the polished black marble of their 1940s sign is so breathtaking, it's been left as-is by every tenant since (429 N Eutaw Street, Baltimore, MD 21201).

44_Graffiti Alley

Tag, you're it

Graffiti is seen by some as a scourge on our cities, a heinous act of vandalism that symbolizes decay and lawlessness. But to many, graffiti is an art form that is more than just tags and spray paint: it's the act of an artist throwing a piece of themselves up on a wall in bombastic glory, a culture of misfits who see the world not in black and white but in vibrant color where everything is a canvas. Unlike most other artists, graffitists understand that their work is ephemeral, just as we all are. You can truly understand this ethos in a hidden L-shaped alley off of Howard Street, just a bit past North Avenue. There are no large signs or marking to lead you there, though be assuaged you are not doing anything wrong by entering.

In fact, no one is: this is the only place in the state of Maryland where graffiti is legal.

Immunity from prosecution isn't the only reason why artists from far and wide travel to Baltimore to leave their mark here. The legal aspect means that artists can take their time creating the piece they want, carefully adding details and shading, test out new styles and techniques. Working in a safe space also provides the sense of community. Many graffitists tend to work alone. Here they can work alongside others out in the open – kindred spirits in a verboten medium forced way underground. This is a place where knowledge is shared, friendships forged.

For the observer, Graffiti Alley is a completely immersive experience – a technicolor fishbowl of Krylon paint. On any given weekend you'll find people conducting impromptu photo shoots or shooting music videos, adding an additional layer of spectacle to an already remarkable space. If you're the type who likes to take their time, the weekdays are best: you'll occasionally find an artist or two working in solitude, and watching them bring their ideas to life is an utterly remarkable experience.

Address Howard Street & W 19 1/2 Street, Baltimore, MD 21201 | **Hours** Unrestricted | **Tip** Ask a local artist where they go for supplies, and the majority will tell you to head to Artist & Craftsman Supply (135 W North Avenue, Baltimore, MD 21201, www.artistcraftsman.com), the creative's version of Candyland. Not only will you find just about anything to make your left-brained dreams come true, but you'll also be happy to know you're spending money at a shop that's 100% employee owned.

45__Highfield House
Our Bauhaus in the middle of our street

Looming over the quiet neighborhood of Tuscany-Canterbury is one of the most stunning works of mid-twentieth-century modernist architecture, designed by a man considered to be one of the pioneers of the form: Ludwig Mies van der Rohe.

Born in Aachen, Germany in 1886, he worked at his father's architectural stone-carving business and then moved to Berlin to apprentice in design. He soon found himself under the tutelage of one of the fathers of architectural reform, Peter Behrens, working alongside other apprentices who would become legends in their own right: Le Corbusier and Bauhaus School founder Walter Gropius.

After the horrors of WWI, Van der Rohe was looking for a way to reconcile the relationship between society, the rapid advancements of modern technology with the beauty of the natural world. The post-war government ushered in a new age of total freedom in the art world, and Germany soon set the artistic tone for the entire 20th century. Eventually Van der Rohe and the Bauhaus School (where he was later president) came to define the emerging genre of modernism, and he is now considered the one of the most influential artistic figures in history.

Van der Rohe accepted less than 10 residential commissions in his lifetime, the Highfield House condominiums being one of them. It exemplifies the modernist ethos of form following function, yet in its simplicity remains indescribably beautiful. Standing 15 stories tall, the behemoth structure floats above the ground on concrete pillars. Its large picture windows were a revolutionary addition at the time and eventually became standard in newer luxury apartment complexes. The lobby walls are floor-to-ceiling windows, allowing one to experience both modernism and nature simultaneously. Considered an architectural triumph, it was added to the National Register of Historic Places in 2007.

Address 4000 N Charles Street, Baltimore, MD 21218 | Hours Viewable from the outside only | Tip If you love Van der Rohe, grab a cab south to One Charles Center (100 North Charles Street, Baltimore, MD 21201, www.onecharlescenter.com), his other (more well-known) Baltimore masterpiece. Built in 1962, it was the city's first modernist building, which kicked off the nationally-recognized urban renewal movement.

46__Hoehn's Bakery
Doughnuts Old World style

If asked to name a food associated with Baltimore, most people would probably say crabs in general, or crabcakes to be specific. A century ago, however, the official food of Baltimore was not crab, but sweet Maryland peaches. Grown up and down the coast, peaches were brought to the city by the millions each year to be shipped across the country. Long before crabcakes were even an idea, peach cake reigned supreme, a lightly sweetened yeast cake with thick peach slices baked into the top, an American adaptation of the traditional apple cake enjoyed by the thousands of German immigrants that made Baltimore their home. How is this a recipe that's been nearly forgotten about? After visiting Hoehn's Bakery, you'll be thankful that one of the last German bakeries still remembers.

There are so many old bakeries that have eschewed the old ways for modern convenience, but not Hoehn's. It sticks out on its corner in Highlandtown, as if it has been transported through time from its opening day in 1927. Founded by immigrant William Hoehn, the business remains in the family, and they still follow his recipes to the letter. Everything is made by hand, using as little machinery as possible, and baked in the original brick-hearth oven that has been used since day one.

You think you're here for peach cake, but in reality you're here for everything. There are no shortcuts, no chemical-laden mixes, no preservatives. Their classic doughnuts, glazed in real chocolate or piped full of light-as-air Swiss meringue, are reminiscent of the ones served by the Salvation Army to soldiers during World War I, origins of the nickname "doughboys." The holidays bring authentic old country specialties, such as hot cross buns at Lent and a superlative stollen come Christmas. By all means, buy one of every item on the menu.

Don't forget the peach cake. You may never consider a crabcake again.

Address 400 S Conkling Street, Baltimore, MD 21224, +1 (410)675-2884, www.hoehnsbakery.com | **Hours** Wed–Sat 7:30am–6pm | **Tip** If Baltimore is stealing your heart (as it tends to do), know that the good people over at Baltimore in a Box will gladly ship survival kits to your house whenever you get a hankering for some local food and Charm City culture (246 S Conkling Street, Baltimore, MD 21224, www.baltimoreinabox.com).

47 — Hoffman Memorial German Library

Preserving the sacred texts

There has been a strong German presence in Baltimore since the 1600s. Pious Lutherans practiced their devotional life in the sanctity of each other's homes, using the Bibles and hymn books they had brought from Germany. Today, you can find those books in the Hoffman Memorial German Library of Zion Church, which houses the congregation that the early settlers secretly founded in 1755.

Over the next two centuries, Germans continued to flock to Baltimore in droves. Heirloom texts were bequeathed to the parish, and many more historic texts were amassed by Julius Hofmann, a pastor who arrived as an assistant in 1889. At the time there were many internal struggles within the church, which fractured the community and led to the alienation of the younger generations, who were heading to other, more modern parishes. Hoffmann's rigorous study of historical Lutheran texts helped him find reconciliation between the old and the new, reorganizing Zion and helping unite with other Lutheran churches that had been put off by older Germanic orthodoxy. Upon his passing in 1928, his enormous personal library was divided, with a small portion of extremely valuable texts, such as the first edition of Martin Luther's Germanic Bible, going to Johns Hopkins University for preservation in the Special Collections Department. The bulk of the collection, over 8,000 manuscripts dating back to 1501, remains in a small library at Zion Church.

The library continues to grow each year, as secular and religious heirlooms are donated by current parishioners and people of German heritage who want to ensure that priceless pieces of their history are preserved. To see the library, you must call ahead to arrange a private viewing.

Address 400 E Lexington Street, Baltimore, MD 21202, +1 (410)727-3939, www.zionbaltimore.org | Hours By appointment only | Tip Sundays from April to December bring Baltimore's biggest farmers market to the area underneath the Jones Falls Expressway. The Sunday Market (E Saratoga Street & Holliday Street, Baltimore, MD 21202, www.baltimarket.org) features artisan food makers, local crafters, musicians, and pop-up restaurants in addition to the farmers, making it more like a party than a simple market.

48__ The Horse You Came In On Saloon

Nevermore for Edgar Allen Poe

It's easy to forget that the charming waterfront of Fell's Point was once a dangerous den of filth and disease, lined with saloons and houses of ill repute, littered with drunken sailors and criminals. The Horse You Came In On Saloon, which opened before the American Revolution, is most famous for being the place where Edgar Allen Poe took his last drink.

It is falsely believed that Poe died from alcoholism and habitual drug use. While he did have occasional bouts of binge drinking and wild excess, these were tempered with long stretches of sobriety. On the evening of October 3, 1849, Election Day in Baltimore, Poe was found in a gutter outside a Fell's Point polling site, delirious, unkempt, and wearing clothes that were not his own. He was brought to a local hospital where he died four days later, never regaining consciousness to explain what had happened to him. The only clue he was able to give was repeatedly screaming out the name "Reynolds" the night before his death.

No one will ever know for sure what happened that night, but one theory could have come straight from Poe's pen. Poe was a well-kept, dapper gentleman, rarely appearing in anything except his trademark black suit. There is a possibility that he was a victim of a form of voter fraud called "cooping," in which gangs who were on the payroll of a political candidate would drug the drinks of unsuspecting bar patrons and then force them to vote multiple times, repeatedly changing their clothes to help disguise their identity. Was Poe targeted that evening in the Horse You Rode in On? Perhaps there were witnesses who knew the truth. A bartender? A fellow drinker? Or maybe the judge who was overseeing the polls of Fell's Point, Henry R. Reynolds?

Address 1626 Thames Street, Baltimore, MD 21231, +1 (410)327-8111, www.thehorsebaltimore.com | **Hours** Daily 11:30am–1:30am | **Tip** A few doors down is Zelda Zen, a longstanding and beloved small business that carries jewelry, gift cards, and other lovely baubles, including unique tiles emblazoned with quirky local sights and icons, made by a local artist. The shop doesn't have a website, but you can follow it on Facebook.

49 _ Hotel Brexton

Mrs. Simpson from poverty to a king's consort

Mount Vernon was home to business magnates, robber barons, and society dames. One young woman from this wealthy neighborhood would create a scandal so enormous that it changed the course of history for Great Britain: Wallis Warfield Simpson.

Wallis' parents were both born to prominent families, but her father, the black sheep of his family, died penniless of tuberculosis when Wallis was an infant, leaving her widowed mother Alice not much more than a few pieces of heirloom silver and a good pedigree. She and her mother were taken in by a wealthy grandmother and an uncle. Uncle Sol was very controlling and madly in love with Alice, who did not return his feelings. So he forced them to live in small quarters and doled out enough money for them to survive. Eventually, Alice saved enough money to move to a boarding house called the Brexton Hotel.

The accommodations were not befitting a mother and daughter who, had their fortunes been different, would have been American royalty. Alice worked constantly for low wages to support them, while their family sat in the lap of luxury only a few blocks away. Despite her moxie, Alice was unable to pay for their room, and they were taken in by Alice's sister Bessie.

Wallis became a relentless social climber, a trait she attributed to her days at the Brexton as a young girl from two prominent families, but alone and impoverished.

She married once and was about to divorce her second husband when she met Prince Edward of Wales through her society connections, and the two fell madly in love. When Edward became king, the British government refused to allow him to marry his once divorced and still married American mistress. In a move that shocked the world, King Edward VIII abdicated the British throne for the woman he loved. They married shortly afterwards, and remained together until death did them part.

Address 868 Park Avenue, Baltimore, MD 21201, +1 (443)478-2100, www.hotelbrexton.com | **Hours** Lobby access during business hours | **Tip** Take a walk to 34 E Preston Street, a private residency, to catch a glimpse of uncle Sol's house.

50__House Of Cards Scenes
Watch your step

You could say the city of Washington, DC is itself a character in Netflix's hit series *House of Cards*. This Emmy- and Golden Globe-winning drama starring Kevin Spacey as diabolical politician Frank Underwood exposes the nefarious underbelly of government, set against the backdrop of a breathtaking city overflowing with American history. Just like many of the things that come out of Frank Underwood's mouth, this is all lies: *House of Cards* does the majority of it's filming in Baltimore.

If you're a fan of the show, you could easily spend an entire weekend seeking places where some of the most memorable (and shocking) TV moments occurred. Head to Bolton Hill, where you can snap a photo of yourself in front of Frank and Claire Underwood's home at 1609 Park Avenue. Reporter Zoe's Barnes' apartment is at 9 E Preston Street in Mount Vernon. The show makes it appear to be on the corner of Danger Street and Murder Avenue, but in reality, it's across the street from a Starbucks. There's a chance you could experience deja vu while visiting many of the city's restaurants, such as Tio Pepe, Golden West Cafe, or Sip & Bite – all places where characters have met up for a bite to eat (or to plot a conspiracy). When it comes to international relations, the Four Seasons Hotel in Harbor East stands in for the United Nations. Head to the Engineer's Club in Mount Vernon if you want to experience what it's like to visit the Kremlin.

Possibly the most shocking moment of the show requires a trip on the Metro to stand in the spot where we learned just how far Frank is willing to go in his quest for power. Go deep underground into the Charles Center Station and walk to the far end of the platform, past the stairs. *[Spoiler Alert]* You're standing on the exact spot where Francis Underwood grabs his lover and unwitting pawn, Zoe Barnes, and pushes her in front of a moving train.

Address Francis and Claire's Home: 1609 Park Avenue, Baltimore, MD 21217; Zoe's Apartment: 6 E Preston Street, Baltimore, MD 21202; Engineer's Club: 11 W Mt Vernon Place, Baltimore, MD 21201 | **Hours** Viewable from the outside only | **Tip** It's surprising that *House of Cards* has yet to film scenes at Chase Court, though you may recognize it from episodes of *Veep* or *The Wire*. This 1879 Gothic former parish house is now a rentable venue for films and photo shoots, and highly popular for Harry Potter and Renaissance-themed weddings (1112 St Paul Street, Baltimore, MD 21202, www.chasecourt.com).

51 Illusions Bar & Theater

Sip slowly and carry a big wand

Spencer Horseman didn't have a choice about becoming an entertainer. His father Ken literally ran away from home to join the circus. He became a clown with Ringling Bros. Barnum and Bailey circus, travelling coast-to-coast delighting young and old, until the day he found love with an acrobat clown named Mary.

They left the glamorous life beneath the big top and returned home to Ken's native Baltimore to start a family. Ken continued working as a clown, becoming the man behind Ronald McDonald's greasepaint for twenty years. They also opened a mom-and-pop magic and joke shop, where Spencer was put to work at the tender age of four. His showbiz genes made him a prodigy, starting with ventriloquism at the age of 8, and by the age of 15 he had already appeared on the *David Letterman Show* and on stage with magical legends like David Copperfield and Lance Burton in Las Vegas.

In 2007, Spencer and Ken converted the old joke shop into Illusions Bar and Theater, where every Friday and Saturday night Spencer wows the crowd with his Vaudeville-style act, while the bar serves cocktails in vintage speakeasy-style glamour. You'll sip on Jazz Age libations underneath dazzling custom chandeliers while tucked into a plush banquette, all while Spencer performs mind-boggling sleight of hand illusions and brings the crowd to the edge of their seats as he dangles upside-down from the ceiling while confined inside a straight jacket. Once your pulse has returned to normal, enjoy the rest of the night listening to the piano player fill the air with 1920s jazz while relaxing on leather sofas. The walls are adorned with antique posters of some of the 20th century's greatest magicians. Don't forget to make reservations first – even though they've been open for over a decade, a night of magic and wonder with Spencer Horseman is still the hottest ticket in town.

Address 1025 S Charles Street, Baltimore, MD 21230, +1 (410)727-5811, www.illusionsmagicbar.com | **Hours** Fri & Sat 5pm–1am | **Tip** The Book Escape (805 Light Street, Baltimore, MD 21230, www.thebookescape.com) is a bibliophile's version of heaven, with used books stacked from floor to ceiling and shelves overflowing into piles on the floor. It also feels as if it never ends, as the building is laid out in railroad style, with even more shelves appearing past where you thought the shop ends.

52 Irish Railroad Workers Museum

The hands that launched the country westward

Carve out some time to visit the B&O Railroad Museum, situated in a tiny 1840s row house. Step in the shoes of the working families who made it possible for the country to move rapidly westward.

The B&O opened in 1830 with Mount Clare Station in what was the countryside. As it incrementally grew, so did the neighborhood around it. Once the Great Famine began in 1845, Irish workers poured into the area. Strips of tiny conjoined row houses were quickly built. Southwest Baltimore transformed from a forest into a tight network of cobblestone streets and alleyways crowded with Irish immigrants. A large public market building was erected on Hollins Street, and St. Peter's Catholic church was built a few blocks down.

But when the railroad closed and the descendants of those immigrants fled the cities for the greener pastures in the suburbs, Pigtown and Hollins Market descended into urban decay. Row houses were abandoned and boarded up; those that were inhabitable were sold for as little as a dollar by the city government. Many Baltimoreans, however, were not ready to allow their history to be erased.

In 1997, locals from the non-profit Railroad Historic District Corp. determined to save a row of condemned alley houses on Lemmon Street that had been slated for demolition. Built in 1840, these meager dwellings are monuments to the poor who lived and died within their walls. Their original interiors were intact: four small rooms with simple Doric fireplaces, a wide kitchen with original hearths and built in shelves, and a tight winding staircase that connects the rooms.

Three are now private residences, but two of the homes have been converted into the Irish Railroad Workers Museum.

Address 918 Lemmon Street, Baltimore, MD 21223, +1 (410)669-8154, www.irishshrine.org |
Hours Fri & Sat 11am–2pm, Sun 1pm–4pm | Tip Hollins Market (26 S Arlington Avenue,
Baltimore, MD 21223, www.bpmarkets.com/markets/hollins-market) was founded in the 1830s
for the booming railroad-worker population and remains the city's oldest market building. The
square itself is undergoing a revitalization of sorts, with excellent restaurants such as Zella's
popping up, and groundbreaking art institutions like the Black Cherry Puppet Theater.

53 John Carroll Crypt

Founding Father of Catholicism in the New World

The province of Maryland was established by Lord Baltimore for those looking to escape persecution from the Church of England. It is often overlooked that Catholics were amongst those seeking a safe haven in the New World. However, their sanctuary didn't last long, as the puritans eventually moved north from Virginia and overthrew the government, outlawing Catholicism and forcing any religious services underground. It wasn't till the end of the American Revolution that the church could begin to reform.

John Carroll was born in Maryland to a Catholic family that had been instrumental in the development of the province. His desire to join the priesthood as a Jesuit brought him to a seminary in France that had been established for exiled Catholics. He remained in Europe until the age of 40, when Pope Clement XIV suppressed the Jesuits, forcing him to flee back to Maryland. There was no church for him to return to, so he worked as a missionary conducting mass in secret. During the war, Catholics were able to surface, but were still without a diocese until 1783, when Carroll and five other Jesuits began establishing the American Catholic Church.

The priests began to petition Rome for a bishop, and were granted their wish. The American clergy was allowed to select the site for their national cathedral and elect their own bishop; they chose Baltimore, and John Carroll as their leader. His first years were focused on building the framework for a national church, as well as establishing institutions of Catholic education: St. Mary's Seminary, and Georgetown University. In 1806, he oversaw the building of the country's first cathedral. He wanted the seat of American Catholicism to be a symbol of a new church for a new country. He laid the cornerstone, but sadly did not live to see its completion. His body became the first interred in the crypt below the cathedral.

Address 409 Cathedral Street, Baltimore, MD 21201, +1 (410)727-3564, www.americasfirstcathedral.org | Hours Mon–Fri 7am–4pm, Sat 8:30am–5:30pm, Sun 7am–4:30pm | Tip Kitty-corner is the main branch of the Enoch Pratt Free Library, which houses the personal artifacts of famed journalist H. L. "The Sage of Baltimore" Menken. In addition, the library's large wing dedicated to African American Studies is not to be missed (400 Cathedral Street, Baltimore, MD 21201, www.prattlibrary.org/locations/central).

54 Junius Brutus Booth Grave
The greatest star of them all

Most all of us daydream of a life of glitz, glamor, and stardom, but fame is fleeting, and legacies can be forgotten. So it is with Junius Brutus Booth, one of the greatest stars of the early 19th century. An English actor whose fame rose to stratospheric heights after his performance of the title role in Richard III at London's Covent Garden Theatre, he had few peers. Booth developed a rabid fan base called "Boothites," who would instigate fights with the fan clubs of other actors. Theater in early 19th century Britain was no joke.

In 1821 Booth abandoned his wife and moved to America with a younger woman. He was soon hired, once again asked to play Richard III, and became the most famous actor in the United States. For the next thirty years, he played to packed houses in the finest stages of America and Europe. Privately, however, he was descending into alcoholism, depression, and, eventually, madness. The father of twelve children, five of them predeceased him – three in 1833 alone when a cholera epidemic swept through Baltimore. To say the rest of his life was erratic would be an understatement He would miss lines, skip performances, and eventually required son Edwin to be his constant companion: handling his finances, cleaning up his messes, and keeping him sober. Edwin too went into show business, becoming himself the greatest star of the late 19th century.

Junius died in 1852 and was buried in the Booth family plot at Greenmount Cemetery, where he would be joined by his wife and seven of his children. It was 13 years after his death that his legacy as an actor would be nearly erased from history, eclipsed by the celebrity of his son – and not the aforementioned Edwin.

The Booth name is now forever associated with his son John Wilkes Booth, an actor like his father before him, and the man who assassinated President Abraham Lincoln.

Address 1501 Greenmount Avenue, Baltimore, MD 21202, +1 (410)539-0641, www.greenmountcemetery.com | Hours Mon–Sat 9am–4pm | Tip It's not on the official map, so you'll need to wander around to spot the grave of inventor Elijah Bond. You won't be able to miss it, as it's built to resemble his most famous creation: the Ouija board.

55_Kinetic Sculpture Race
Gators and duckies and poodles, oh my!

You don't often see a 15-foot pink poodle/unicorn hybrid coasting through the Baltimore Harbor, or witness ten adults dressed as bees pedaling a papier-mâché hive through a pit of mud. And indeed, there is only one day where this is likely to happen: the annual East Coast National Championship Kinetic Sculpture race, held every May by the American Visionary Art Museum (AVAM).

Kinetic sculpture is a human-powdered work of art meant for racing, and this race is *all-terrain*: 15 miles of water, sand, mud, and asphalt. Made by hand from spare parts, junked bicycles, and upcycled trash, competing sculptures must adhere to a very strict set of rules: they must be powered by human pedaling with no pushing or pulling allowed; they must remain completely above water with no pilot exceeding 8% of total body/clothing wetness; each sculpture must carry "one comforting item of psychological luxury," which is defined as a sock puppet made "from a not-too-recently-worn sock from the home." This is a very well thought out competition.

Calling everyone a winner is hardly satisfying for such a competition, but you have to admit – any team that can make a functional kinetic sculpture really deserves acknowledgment. Competitors vie for 14 titles, like the Golden Dinosaur Award for most memorable vehicular breakdown, or the Next to Last Award. It doesn't always pay to come in first: the team that finishes smack dab in the middle is the winner of the Mediocre Award and becomes eligible to compete in the World Championships in California, where the grand prize is promised also to be highly mediocre.

Not in town for the race? That will not be a problem. Simply visit AVAM to see some of their most memorable (and still standing) sculptures. If you'd like to try your hand at entering yourself one day, their website will give you all the tips and tricks you need to sail into ludicrous glory.

Address 800 Key Highway, Baltimore, MD 21230, +1 (410)244-1900, www.avam.org | **Hours** Tue–Sun 10am–6pm | **Tip** Staring at the beautiful Inner Harbor can give you the urge to grab a boat and sail off towards the horizon. There's a place that can teach you how to do just that: the Downtown Sailing Center (1425 Key Highway, Suite 110, Baltimore, MD 21230, www.downtownsailing.org) at the Baltimore Museum of Industry, where aspiring and seasoned sailors come together to take on the waterways of the Chesapeake.

56___Krakus Deli

Addictively delicious meats

The sign at Krakus Deli reads "The Best Polish Deli on the East Coast," and while the claim might come across as bombastic, it would be tremendously hard to make a case against it. All you need to do is to step into its tiny storefront and take a few sniffs. Talk to the kindly, charming, and gregarious owner, and he'll humbly tell you that anyone can make sausage. Sure, *technically* this is true. But can anyone make sausage quite like he does? Not a chance.

At one time, much of Southeast Baltimore was nicknamed "Little Poland," thanks to the high numbers of Polish immigrants coming to work on the docks and in factories. Their imprint remains: from the towering gold Katyn Massacre Memorial in Harbor East to the Pulaski Monument in Patterson Park.

The days of strolling the streets of Canton without hearing a single word of English spoken are over, and most of the Polish shops and restaurants closed years ago, but still Krakus remains, and the moment you step through the door you'll see, or rather, smell why. This is one of the only shops on the East Coast that's still legally allowed to smoke their meat in-house, which fills the air of the tiny storefront with a thick, porky perfume. Behind the counter, you'll find dozens of different pork sausages dangling from hooks, all tasting dramatically different thanks to the variations of spice and smoke that only a true artist can master.

The signs are mostly in Polish, but the staff are glad to translate – they say that close to 70% of their customers are now foodies who travel from far and wide for such specialties as *myśliwska*, *swojska*, or their legendary *Polska szynka gotowana*, aka "bacon-stuffed bacon." And while you're there, make sure to stock up on some of the imported specialties that line the walls from top to bottom. After all, man cannot live on sausage alone (he also needs chocolate). Pick up a variety horseradish products too, to spark up your palate.

Address 1737 Fleet Street, Baltimore, MD 21231, +1 (410)732-7533, www.krakusdelibaltimore.com | Hours Tue – Fri 10am – 6pm, Sat 9am – 6pm, Sun 10am – 2pm | Tip If you can't wait till you get home to sink your teeth into some Polish food, head into the Broadway Market and seek out Sophia's Place (1640 Aliceanna Street, Baltimore, MD 21231, www.sophiaspolishdeli.com), where you'll be served some of the finest Polish home cooking this side of the Vistula.

57 Lord Baltimore Hotel

Professor Plum, with the knife, in the speakeasy

The Lord Baltimore lives up to its reputation as one of the East Coast's most remarkable historic hotels. Since it opened in 1928, hundreds of celebrities and dignitaries have passed through its timeless art-deco lobby and danced in its opulent ballroom, home to some of the most riotous society parties of the 20th century. This hotel is full of secrets. One is about a haunting. As legend has it, during the Depression, a man and woman who had lost their fortune jumped to their deaths after one final society gala, taking with them their 7-year-old daughter Molly, whom guests have seen wandering the halls and rolling a red ball. Her parents have been spied dancing in the ballroom.

The ballroom is covered with hand-painted murals of Old Baltimore – originals from the 1928 opening. They seem to clash with the overall aesthetic of the hotel which, while historic, is decorated with contemporary furnishing and modern art, thanks to the famous art-collecting family that owns it: the Rubells. As with the other boutique hotels they own, the walls and guest rooms are decorated with pieces from their private collection, with "the exhibition" changing several times a year.

When the Rubells purchased the hotel in 2014 and began renovations, they found something odd behind a wall in the dining room: an honest to goodness speakeasy that had been built in for the 1928 opening. When Prohibition was repealed in 1933, the room was sealed up and forgotten about, staying perfectly preserved, from the fixtures to the silverware, completely in tact. Most of the space was built out to add an extended bar to the hotel restaurant, but there is a secret door on the far left side of the mirrored back wall that leads to a secret lounge. Take the elevator to the 19th floor, where you'll find one of the city's only rooftop bars with stunning views of Downtown and the Inner Harbor.

Address 20 W Baltimore Street, Baltimore, MD 21201, +1 (855)539-1928, www.lordbaltimorehotel.com | Hours Lobby access during business hours | Tip On the corner is the Kimpton Monaco (2 N Charles Street, Baltimore, MD 21201, www.monaco-baltimore.com), which now occupies the former B&O Railroad headquarters. The marble lobby staircase is a vision, and the ground-floor restaurant pours a damn fine martini.

58 Lovely Lane Museum
Birthplace of the Methodist Church

Founded by Anglican priest John Wesley, the Methodists were early advocates of social justice. Wesley visited Georgia in 1736, then a British colony, and became adamant about using the power of God to abolish the slave trade. Though Methodists were still a part of the Church of England, Wesley and his followers were relentlessly persecuted by the government and the clergy. Yet still, they persevered. Societies multiplied, missionaries were dispatched across Europe and into the New World. The chasm between the Methodist movement and the Anglican Church widened, the American missions spread like wildfire, to the point where the movement needed to become a church.

The first Lovely Lane Chapel was built by missionaries in Baltimore in 1774. During the Revolution, they regularly petitioned Wesley to send over more ordained preachers, as missionaries could not baptize those wishing to convert. They pleaded for the right to separate officially into their own church so they could continue growing their ranks. Though Methodism had not officially split from the Church of England into its own entity, John Wesley granted their request. The word was sent to preachers far and wide by horseback, telling them to assemble in Baltimore on Christmas Day. On December 25th, 1784, the Methodist Episcopal Church – now the third-largest denomination in America – was established.

A century later, a new, grander church was built for the birthplace of Methodism. Designed by famed architect Stanford White, it was inspired by the great Byzantine-Romanesque basilicas of Italy and is a remarkable study in design – fitting for such an important and sacred place. The most striking feature is the domed ceiling that hovers above its parishioners: a painted sky full of stars, aligned exactly as they were at 3am on November 6, 1887, the time the church was officially dedicated.

Address 2200 St Paul Street, Baltimore, MD 21218, +1 (410)889-4458, www.lovelylanemuseum.com | Hours Thu & Fri 10am–4pm | Tip The only place any serious musician in Baltimore goes for their guitars is Brothers Music (2112 N Charles Street, Baltimore, MD 21218, www.brothersmusicbaltimore.com), a 3-minute walk from Lovely Lane Chapel. This store is staffed with true experts who will give you the sort of experience chain music stores only dream of offering, which is why skilled guitarists from near and far go out of the way to do their shopping here.

59__The Magic Farting Post
Pull my finger, artistically

It doesn't matter how old you are or how fancy you may be, everyone farts. Whether for sweet relief or a hilarious mishap, farts are the great equalizer that knows neither class nor sense of propriety. Yes we treat them like a shameful secret – going to great (uncomfortable) lengths to not release a glass-shattering blast of thunder, stifling giggles to retain the visage of a mature adult. But if everybody farts, then why not celebrate it?

Bob Bowman is the visionary artist and avant-garde genius behind the Magic Farting Post at the American Visionary Art Museum (AVAM). Captivated by the sparkling quality of mirrors, he began using them as a medium to create magnificent sculptures that eventually caught the attention of the museum's director. His first collaboration was *The Universal Tree of Life*, a magnificent mirrored tree that stands outside the entrance.

He then approached the museum with his idea for his ode to the odorous. The request was a no-brainer for the world's most eccentric museum, and now it may be their most famous piece. You could say that it is Baltimore's very own Mona Lisa – perhaps a highly apt comparison, as that smile could certainly be the sign of a very, *ahem*, *relieved* woman.

It would be a disservice to you if the *Magic Farting Post* were described in too great of detail. It has everything you would want in an interactive farting experience, minus the stink. The post itself is surrounded with curved walls covered with mirrored tile, like a disco-era grotto of passed gas depicting titans of toots and fantastic acts of flatulence. A button emits sounds of accomplished "flautists" (yes, accomplished farters have a legitimate title) as they vie for a title in professional competition (yes, they actually exist). There is no shame in breaking into an uncontrollable fit of giggles – odds are, everyone around you will be doing the same.

Address 800 Key Highway, Baltimore, MD 21230, +1 (410)244-1900, www.avam.org | **Hours** Tue–Sun 10am–6pm | **Tip** If you're visiting the AVAM anyway, you must visit Sideshow, the museum shop that redefines your expectation of what "exit through the gift shop" should mean. It's filled top to bottom with things you never knew you wanted but you absolutely need: obscure bobbleheads, sacrilegious knickknacks, profane coloring books, bizarre fashion accessories, and a functioning original Zoltar Machine.

60_Make Studio
Art with purpose

Depending on whom you speak with, "Outsider Art" is either a beautiful or derogatory term. Technically, the phrase refers to art created by those who do not receive any formal training, so some find it dismissive. In Baltimore, being an outsider artist is seen as possibly the highest form of compliment. This is not a town where art belongs to the 1 percent – it is something that belongs to everyone. Up north in the bohemian neighborhood of Hampden is a studio that exemplifies these beliefs and churns out some of the most remarkable (and affordable) outsider artwork you're likely to come across.

Make Studio provides a space for artists with disabilities to create, discover, and express themselves. Founded in 2010 by several individuals with backgrounds in art therapy and education, what began as a small project has grown into a thriving art space and gallery where close to thirty "outsiders" come each week to work on projects. One of the remarkable aspects of this studio is their ethos: it is not just a space for therapy, but a place to celebrate the individual – to give them a voice to communicate that they are more than just "people with disabilities," but brilliant human beings whose talents are distinct and unique.

Art has other benefits besides just creating. Working in the studio allows the artists to develop greater self-sufficiency, as they have the freedom to pursue the arts through their own passions, picking their own topics and mediums and curating a workspace all their own. They sell their artwork through the ground-floor gallery and Maker's website, which not only generates income, but shows them how their art not only brings them joy, but brings it to others as well. When you purchase a remarkable piece of art from Make Studio, you are affirming that the art world is an inclusive place where everyone belongs, and everyone's voice is important.

Address 3326 Keswick Road, Baltimore, MD 21211, +1 (443)627-3502, www.make-studio.org | **Hours** Tue–Fri 9:30am–4pm, Sat 10:30am–1:30pm, and by appointment | **Tip** Jill Andrews' eponymous bridal atelier offers bespoke gowns sewn on site from her own patterns, and also creates couture gowns for the bride who wants to look like no other. Her most famous outfit, however, is not bridal – she, along with researchers at Johns Hopkins, designed the hazmat suits for doctors treating the Ebola endemic (3355 Keswick Road, Suite 101, Baltimore, MD 21211, www.jillandrewsgowns.com).

61 McFadden Art Glass

Handling fire and ice

If you search for glassblowing videos on the Internet, it's easy to lose yourself for hours (or days). Though they make it look easy, the greatest artisans of glass spend years – decades even – perfecting their craft through intense training and practice. On the fringes of the Highlandtown arts district you'll find such a master. It's worth a visit to his studio just to watch him work or ogle one of his many mind-blowing pieces, particularly the technicolor Murrini patterns. But what really makes this place a "must visit" is the opportunity to try glassblowing yourself, under the wing of master craftsman Tim McFadden.

McFadden fell in love with glassblowing as a college student, and he won a grant through his university to transform that love into a business. His business plan created many avenues to grow as an artist and entrepreneur, teaching being one of them. While his daily work throughout the years has helped him grow, the moments in between his own projects when he opens his studio to others is what he cites as a driving force in his artistry. "The best part about teaching is seeing the glass through the eyes of a beginner. You can feel their excitement and see their face light up when you pull that first molten glob of glass from the furnace."

If you remain apprehensive about trying your skills within a medium that reaches an utterly terrifying 2,000°F (1,100°C), or you are simply nervous because of a self-perceived lack of talent, understand that there is no "right" demographic to take a class. McFadden is open and eager to welcome anyone who comes through his doors with a mind full of curiosity. "We have had kindergarten field trips followed by retirement communities. We had car clubs followed by bachelorette parties, and so on. No one that comes through and visits the shop leaves here without a smile on their face."

Address 6802 Eastern Avenue, Baltimore, MD 21224, +1 (410)631-6039, www.mcfaddenartglass.com | Hours Tue–Sat noon–8pm, Sun noon–5pm | Tip Diners are the quintessential establishments where America really eats, though they are not all created equal. One that is head and shoulders above the rest is the Broadway Diner, which, with it's friendly service 24 hours a day, excellent food, and spotless decor, makes it the kind of joint that sets the bar for the rest (6501 Eastern Avenue, Baltimore, MD 21224, www.broadwaydiner1.com).

62 Michael Phelps Swim Center

Go for the gold

Charm City loves its sports heroes, but they take an extra shine to one local boy who represents the best of Baltimore as he grew up to become not only the greatest athlete who has ever competed in his sport, but one who many consider to be the greatest swimmer of all time: 23-time Olympic gold medalist Michael Phelps.

Born and raised in the Baltimore area, Phelps' started taking swimming lessons at the age of seven. Nature designed him physically to be the world's greatest swimmer, from his 6' 4" frame to his very large feet. His ankles are also double jointed, allowing him to point them beyond even the range of a ballet dancer, more like fins than feet. He was diagnosed with ADHD, just like Baltimore's other favorite son Babe Ruth, which not only can be treated effectively with lots of physical activity, but also causes periods of hyper focus during comforting activities. Add all these things up, and you have a swimmer who is more or less unstoppable.

Meadowbrook Aquatic Center in Mount Washington has been home to an elite swim team since 1968, one that has been called an "Olympic machine" as it has sent at least one swimmer to every summer games since 1984. Phelps set a national record for his age group at age 10 and began training privately with senior coach Bob Bowman. He began setting more national records, many of which still stand, and at the age of 15 he became the youngest male swimmer in over 60 years to be sent to the Olympics.

He concluded his final Olympic games in 2016 as the most decorated champion ever, with 28 total medals, 23 of them gold. He lived in Baltimore, training at Meadowbrook, throughout his entire storied career. That swimming school is now called the Michael Phelps Swim School, offering classes to all ages and all skill levels.

Address 5700 Cottonworth Avenue, Baltimore, MD 21209, +1 (410)433-8300, www.mpswimschool.com | **Hours** Mon–Fri 5:30am–8pm, Sat 6am–8pm, Sun 10am–8pm; subject to change during the winter season | **Tip** The jaw-droppingly gorgeous home of a Gilded Age railroad tycoon John W. Garrett, the Evergreen House, is now an intimate museum and library displaying the princely private collections of its original inhabitants: Asian antiquities, ancient manuscripts, impressionist art, and beyond (4545 N Charles Street, Baltimore, MD 21210, www.museums.jhu.edu/evergreen.php).

63 Mobtown Ballroom

Dance the night away!

Got ten bucks in your pocket and looking for a good time? Put on your dancing shoes, and then jump and jive down to Pigtown, where you can dance the night away at Mobtown Ballroom – the hottest swing dance club on the East Coast. A floor full of people doing jitterbug and lindy hop may seem anachronistic, but this city has a thriving underground scene of retro fanatics whose hard work and moxie made a haven like this happen.

It began with three young college grads looking for a permanent spot for their swinging subculture: as you can imagine, joints like this ain't around like they used to be, and dancers are used to travelling far and wide for a good night out. Falling into the laps of Mobtown's owners was a perfectly imperfect spot: a dilapidated church built in 1870, located in the historic Pigtown neighborhood. Relying on the kindness of friends and strangers, they restored the building with what they call "a ridiculous amount of volunteer labor." Every bit of cash they could scrape together went into building the Church of Swing, and by opening night they were flat broke. Doors were open with fingers crossed, and by the end of the week it was met with a flood of dancing shoes: Mobtown Ballroom was a bona fide hit.

Don't know a thing about that East Coast Swing? Not a problem. Dance nights are preceded by drop-in classes where every skill level is welcome, and on any given night you'll see plenty of beginners having a ball right next to the advanced dancers wowing the wallflowers with gravity-defying moves. The calendar has expanded to offer other niche programming, such as live blues and rockabilly bands, and classes in the aerial arts. Other clubs might be places to pick up chicks or to try too hard to look cool, but at Mobtown, the only point of going out is to have some fun, make new friends, and dance like there's no tomorrow.

Address 861 Washington Boulevard, Baltimore, MD 21230, +1 (443)699-3040, www.mobtownballroom.com | Hours Dances, Fri & Mon 7:30pm; check website for class schedule | Tip If you need to find some killer vintage duds to dance like your life depends on it, head up to the Hunting Ground (3649 Falls Road, Baltimore, MD 21211, www.shophuntingground.com) another repurposed old church that specializes in antique fashions as well as pieces from up-and-coming local designers.

64 Moon Landing Evidence
Debunking the age-old conspiracy theories

One of the biggest conspiracy theories of the 20th century is still hotly debated today: did man actually land on the moon, or was the entire thing faked on a Hollywood soundstage by the CIA? There's most certainly enough compelling evidence out there to make that claim, like "confessions" by cameramen who claim they were on set, or reports written by armchair intellectuals that attempt to discredit the science. The smoking gun to all of this truth seeking, of course, is the photographs and video feed supplied by NASA itself, which shows inconsistencies that seem to corroborate all these outlandish theories – inconsistencies are explained at the National Electronics Museum, where the actual recording equipment is displayed.

The story of how the inconsistencies came to exist is so outlandish that it requires a book (or screenplay) all of its own. It involves a bad connection, a television in a remote station in the Australian outback, a group of careless engineers who recorded over nearly all of the originals, a lost master reel, a rental storage garage, and a large hole that was dug deep in the woods of West Virginia on land owned by an anti-government survivalist – all quite fascinating material to conspiracy theorists. The evidence of how mankind's greatest achievement came to be the target of sensationalism is right there in the museum, where you can not only observe the lunar camera and the terrestrial broadcaster, but also see dozens of other formerly-classified artifacts that have been used by the government to map the cosmos and monitor the world around us.

This is a small museum staffed by a passionate staff who live for this level of geekery, so don't hesitate to ask any and all questions about the collection. Chances are you'll get a history lesson more insane than you ever expected… that is, if our shadow government of lizardmen allows them to tell it.

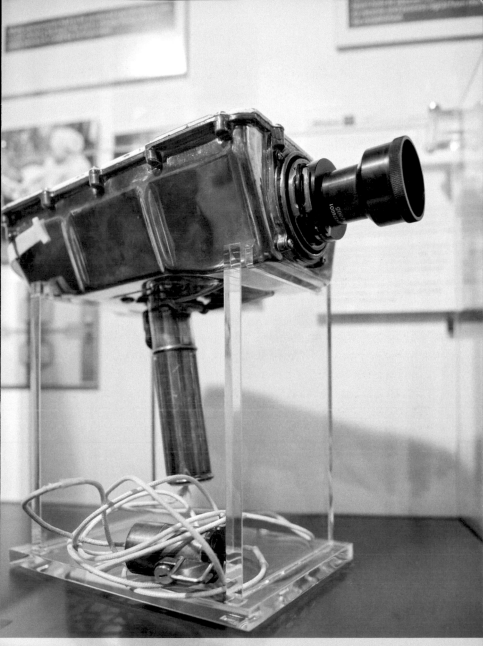

Address 1745 W Nursery Road, Linthicum Heights, MD 21090, +1 (410)765-0230, www.nationalelectronicsmuseum.org | Hours Mon–Fri 9am–4pm, Sat 10am–2pm | Tip What's better than crabs? Crabs and video games! Crabtowne USA does double duty as a friendly and affordable seafood restaurant and an old-school arcade with over 70 cabinet classics and 21 vintage pinball machines (1500 Crain Highway South, Glen Burnie, MD 21061, www.crab-towne.com).

65__Most Literal Bus Stop
You may want to miss the next crosstown

If you're looking to grab the 013 Bus on Eastern Avenue in High-landtown, it's not too hard to figure out where to wait. Right off the corner of South East Avenue are three giant sculptures measuring 14 feet high and 7 feet wide: a *B*, a *U*, and an *S*.

This bus stop is built with steel and planks of wood, just as most municipal benches are. The heavy frame prevents it from being vandalized, and it supports a good amount of weight. Several people can fit inside each letter in various positions, shielding themselves from the sun on a hot day, or staying dry in a torrential thunderstorm.

You can't help cracking a smile at the *BUS* stop, which was designed by the Madrid-based art collective mmmm…. Unveiled in 2014, this functional piece of public art was part of the TRANSIT: Creative Placemaking With Europe in Baltimore project – an exchange program that allowed European artists to cross the pond and change landscapes in American cities. The concept of "Creative Placemaking" is not merely about beautifying public spaces, but creating works that are human-centric and locally inspired, and that invite the community to communicate with each other through them.

BUS certainly provokes the imagination. On any given day, you can find people of all ages gleefully engaging in impromptu photo shoots with their camera phones. Children and teenagers climb the sides and bounce off the walls – and occasionally you'll see a few adults giving in to their inner child to join the fun. You'll find people sitting on the edges waiting patiently, or comfortably sprawled out in the letters' curves. When something that is normally drab and boring becomes both quirky and functional, it instantly transforms into a conversation piece that inspires total strangers to have fun with it together. *BUS* brings delight into a normally forgettable part of your daily routine.

Address Corner of South East Avenue and Eastern Avenue, Baltimore, MD 21224 |
Hours Unrestricted | Tip *BUS* sits outside the Creative Alliance, a rehabbed 1930 movie
palace that is now home to an artistic collective, featuring a gallery, concerts, unique
performances, public workshops, and so much more (3134 Eastern Avenue, Baltimore,
MD 21224, www.creativealliance.org).

66 Mount Auburn Cemetery
History shall not be forgotten

While Baltimore has a recorded history of abolitionism and civil rights activism, it also has a shameful history of discrimination and segregation, which is often left unaddressed. Most slaves were never given the dignity of a proper burial; free blacks and whites were not permitted to be buried in the same cemeteries.

It is said that the Mount Auburn Cemetery was established on land that had been used to bury former slaves as early as 1810, at which time it was thick woodlands and well off the beaten path. In 1868 it was claimed as an official burial ground by the black community, and in 1872, Sharp Street United Methodist Church (see ch. 90) officially signed a deed of ownership. It was officially sanctified and dedicated as the "City of the Dead for Colored People," the only cemetery that would allow the burial of African Americans.

During the 20th century, Mount Auburn slowly declined into a state of utter disrepair. With the cost of maintenance rising, Sharp Street couldn't afford the most basic of care. Weeds and grass grew so tall that the few headstones that had not been destroyed became completely invisible. Even today, there are places where caskets have begun to peek through the ground. Many sections had become completely inaccessible due to overgrowth.

In recent years, however, Mount Auburn has seen significant improvements, thanks to the efforts of a unique rehabilitation program for prison inmates. The cemetery was rededicated in 2012, once again restoring dignity to the people buried there.

It is worthwhile to visit to pay respect to many whom history has forgotten, as well as those who have made indelible contributions to American history yet had their final resting places lost to view: mother of the Civil Rights Movement Lillie Mae Carroll Jackson, the first black lightweight boxing champion Joseph Gans, and hundreds of unnamed slaves.

Address 2630 Waterview Avenue, Baltimore, MD 21230, +1 (410)547-0337, www.mountauburn.org | Hours Daily 8am–8pm | Tip Head east to find the largest expanse of natural shoreline in the Baltimore Harbor: Middle Branch Park (3301 Waterview Avenue, Baltimore, MD 21230, www.bcrp.baltimorecity.gov/parks/ middle-branch). Depending on the time of year, you'll be able to fish, crab, and kayak, or jump on the first leg of the Gwynns Falls Hiking Trail.

67 __ Mr. Trash Wheel

The hero we all need

The biggest celebrity in Baltimore at the moment isn't a person, but an amphibious trash-collection vehicle with large googly eyes and a rabid social media presence. We're talking about the King of the Harbor, the Grand Poobah of Garbage: Mr. Trash Wheel.

Born in the spring of 2014, Mr. Trash Wheel is stationed at the mouth of the Jones Falls River, gobbling all debris that comes its way before it can flow out into the Chesapeake Bay. The first of his kind, Mr. Trash Wheel has been so successful that he's already spawned Professor Trash Wheel, and will soon have kin across the globe in Singapore, Bali, and Rio de Janeiro.

Most of what he catches is litter from all across the city, which ends up flowing down storm drains and into the river. The current turns the wheel, which lifts the trash from the water onto a conveyor belt, which dumps it onto a barge to be hauled away and incinerated, which then produces electricity. By the age of one, he had already eaten close to six million cigarette butts; by the age of two, over one million pounds of garbage. He has also caught more than a few bizarre things, most memorably a live python.

What has taken Mr. Trash Wheel from a simple environmental savior to a worldwide phenomenon is his comical social media presence. It began when a short video of him operating in a rainstorm went viral, being viewed nearly 1.5 million times. Realizing they had a star on their hands, the Waterfront Partnership quickly stationed a 24-hour camera on their ingénue, partnered with a creative studio to help bring him to life and give him his famous pair of googly eyes. He's hosted several hilarious Reddit AMAs that are as informative as they are funny. Mr. Trash Wheel has tens of thousands of followers on various social media platforms, who come for the jokes and sardonic wit and end up with a new appreciation for the local ecosystem.

Address Jones Falls Expressway, Baltimore, MD 21202, +1 (410)779-5308 | Hours Unrestricted | Tip Speaking of wit, the lux Wit & Wisdom Tavern in the Four Seasons Hotel has what many consider to be the best brunch buffet in Baltimore. It's a tad on the pricey side, but when you consider the caliber of the food (all you can eat!) and unparalleled harbor side dining, you might agree that it's actually a total steal (200 International Drive, Baltimore, MD 21202, www.witandwisdombaltimore.com).

68 __ Nature Art In Leakin Park

Nature versus nurture

Leakin Park was designed by the famed Olmsted landscape architecture firm, but is the polar opposite of their other projects like Patterson Park across the city. It takes its cues from the northern end of the most famous Olmstead project – New York City's Central Park – which was left virtually untouched by human hands, so that the wilderness that preceded human settlement could break through the crowded metropolis and continue to thrive.

Over a century later, the Maryland Institute College of Art built upon the original vision, conceptualizing an art show of pieces inspired by the environment, and installed along the Gwynns Falls Trail – a major hiking route and waterway that spans the entire city north to south. Years after the exhibition closed, featured artist Doug Retzler approached the board of Leakin Park and suggested the project be revived with a few major twists. First, artwork would be created from materials that were growing within the park so that they would seem as if they were a natural part of the environment. The artworks would also be moved from the Gwynns Falls Trail to the more secluded woodland trails, giving them a hidden quality, like buried treasure to be discovered by hikers. The curators estimate that at least 50% of their first-time visitors have stumbled upon Nature Art in the Park completely by accident (your author included), eliciting mixed responses. Some catch on that it's intentionally created artwork and are absolutely delighted by its inventiveness and beauty.

If you're worried about getting lost (or have an overactive imagination afraid of ghost stories), Nature Art in the Park has several events during the year that feature guided tours and participatory classes on how to make your own art from nature. Otherwise, head to the tennis court where you can grab a map, and set off on your own treasure hunt.

Address 4921 Windsor Mill Road, Gwynn Oak, MD 21207, +1 (410)396-3835, www.facebook.com/NatureArtInThePark | Hours Daily dawn–dusk | Tip To those who aren't aware the gallery exists, the random structures of dangling sticks and twister brambles can elicit sheer terror – which is understandable. The reaction may come less from surprise as eerie familiarity, as parts of the classic horror movie *The Blair Witch Project* were filmed here.

69__Nepal House Restaurant
Elvis has left the Himalayas

Baltimore has plenty of secrets: secret stories, secret tunnels, and some people even have secret lives. Consider Prem Raja Mahat. Doting husband. Successful restaurateur. Co-founder of the Baltimore Association of Nepalese in America. And a rock star so beloved in the Himalayas, he's nicknamed "The Bob Dylan of Katmandu" and "Elvis of the Himalayas."

Mahat is a singer-songwriter who plays *lok geet*, a form of traditional Himalayan folk music. His love of music spanned far beyond the borders of Nepal, and he sought out recordings from all over the world. He had a particular affinity for traditional American country music. Though he couldn't speak a word of English, he was able to understand the intentions behind the notes, finding deep similarities between the music of the Himalayas and that of the Appalachia. After moving to the U.S., he began collaborating with traditional Americana and bluegrass musicians but stayed loyal to lok geet, returning to Nepal multiple times to continue his recording career. Currently, he has 58 full-length albums.

You'll find that showmanship and charisma at Nepal House, the restaurant he owns with his wife in Mount Vernon. Mahat is seen most days warmly welcoming customers with a big smile, treating diners like they're guests in his own home. The menu offers many Indian dishes familiar to American diners, but skip all that in favor of the section that says "Nepali Specialties." An order of momos is a must – flavor packed steamed dumpling that can quickly become an obsession. Share the Thakali Thali, a sampler platter of sorts that will allow you to taste a variety of dishes that are staples in Kathmandu. If you're apprehensive about new flavors, don't hesitate to ask Mahat for guidance. He's been a proud ambassador of his culture worldwide for most of his life. Maybe, if you're really lucky, you can get him to sing a song or two, just for you.

Address 920 N Charles Street, Baltimore, MD 21201, +1 (410)547-0001,
www.nepalhousebaltimore.com | Hours Mon–Thu 11am–2:30pm & 5pm–10pm,
Fri 11am–2:30pm & 5pm–11pm, Sat 11:30am–3pm & 5pm–11pm, Sun 11:30am–3pm &
5pm–10pm | Tip Up on the second floor of an historic townhouse you'll find An Die Musik
(409 N Charles Street, 2nd Floor, Baltimore, MD 21201, www.andiemusiklive.com) an
intimate space for classical, jazz, and world music artists. The space is intimate enough that
you'll feel as if you're at the home of a friend, and the tickets are quite affordable.

70__Nepenthe Homebrew Shop
All natural and much better than kale

With ready-made kits and countless instructional websites, anyone can start brewing beer right in their home. If you've ever tasted a friend's homebrew, you probably know that just because some people "could," doesn't mean that they "should." Point them to Nepenthe Homebrew, located in a historic mill building on the banks of the Jones Falls in Woodberry.

You could be forgiven if you like to pretend that Nepenthe is your own personal brewery, even if you don't know your ale from your lager. Hops gives the beer its flavor, malted grains give it color, then yeasts, sugars, malt extracts… it's predictably complicated, but under the tutelage of the Nepenthe staff, you'll quickly gain the confidence you need to tackle your first batch. Once you've selected the ingredients for your secret formula, you can fill your trunk with all the supplies you'll need to produce in your own home: a kit if you want to dabble, or a fully customized set up if you know you're in it to win it. And if you don't have a spare room to convert into an alehouse, Nepenthe has you covered with a homebrew setup on site, which you can use to brew, ferment, bottle, and keg your own beers. You can even pay them to sherpa you through the process until you're ready to take the training wheels off.

This is also your winemaking headquarters where you can find all the carboys, hydrometers, and siphons you'll need (just add grapes). Come autumn, transform apples into hard cider. Or kick it old-old-old school by brewing up some mead and becoming the most popular guy at the Renaissance fair.

There are lots of other ways to get your DIY on here. Brewing up some kombucha, brine some pickles, or search for scoby to make your own vinegar. And wine and beer are supposed to be good for you too, right? So Nepenthe is a homebrew *and* health-food store, where everything tastes better than kale smoothies.

Address 3600 Clipper Mill Road, 130A, Baltimore, MD 21211, +1 (443)438-4846, www.nepenthehomebrew.com | Hours Mon & Wed–Fri 11am–8pm, Sat 10am–6pm, Sun noon–6pm | Tip If you can't wait a month to taste your own beer, then head to the Waverly Brewing Company (1625 Union Avenue, Baltimore, MD 21211, www.waverlybrewingcompany.com), which is as beloved for its boisterous events, patio lounging, and friendly clientele as it is for its exceptional, often limited-edition microbrews.

71 Nutshell Studies of Unexplained Death

Murder in miniature

Frances Glessner Lee is known as the mother of forensic science. Born in 1878 to a wealthy industrialist father, she was denied a college education. She began to develop an interest in the forensic sciences, but attempts at pursuing the field were rebuffed by her family. Once her brother died and she was left as sole heir to her family's fortune, she finally began pursuing her dream at the age of 52. Using her inheritance, Lee founded the Harvard Associates of Police Science, which operate the Frances Glessner Lee Homicide School today.

In the 1940s, Lee used her artistic abilities to create The Nutshell Studies of Unexplained Death, twenty scale dioramas recreating actual crime scenes. An obsessive perfectionist, she overlooked no detail: cabinets open to reveal their contents, keys turn in their locks. Every piece of paper was carefully replicated by hand.

The dioramas were actually used to train crime scene investigators in the art of looking for clues. At the time, police would often accidentally contaminate crime scenes, not yet understanding that small details could ultimately be significant to solving a case. Twice a year, seminars would be held where officers would be given 90 minutes to analyze the miniature scene using only a magnifying glass and a flashlight, honing their skills of deduction.

Today, the 18 surviving dioramas have been fully restored and are on display on the fourth floor of the Maryland Medical Examiner's Office. They continue to be used as training tools for the Baltimore Police Department. Ms. Lee is a legend in the field and also an artistic muse: she is said to have been the inspiration for the beloved character of Jessica Fletcher on the classic TV show, *Murder, She Wrote.*

Address 900 W Baltimore Street, Baltimore, MD 21223, +1 (410)333-3250 | **Hours** Mon–Fri 8am–5pm | **Tip** As long as you're spooked, why not head over to the home of the master of horror himself, Edgar Allan Poe? This tiny house was his home from 1833 to 1835, and where he wrote his earliest published short stories, as well as his only play, *Politian* (203 N Amity Street, Baltimore, MD 21223, www.poeinbaltimore.org).

72_Observatory at the Maryland Science Center

Where no man has gone before

It's easy to forget that we're all just small specks on a tiny planet hurdling through space – an utterly infinitesimal dot floating in the vastness of an endless universe. Baltimore has just the place for you to be able to stare directly into the expanse and contemplate your existence: the Maryland Science Center Observatory.

The observatory is a staff-only facility most days, and isn't easy to find – in fact, most locals don't even know about this 100% free public program, so crowding is rarely an issue. The front entrance closes at 5pm, so make your way around the back of the building to one marked "groups and tours," head on in and let the folks at the counter know why you're there (there's no secret code word to get into the observatory, but you can make one up if you're so inclined). Once the clock strikes 5:30pm you'll be escorted into an employee elevator that will take you up to the top floor, and then onto a secret terrace where the second best view in Baltimore has been hiding in plain sight for decades.

Up a narrow outdoor staircase is the best view: the Milky Way, as seen through the lens of a gigantic telescope from the 1920s. Your guides to the heavens are normally volunteers who sign up for the job because of their unbridled enthusiasm for the stars: there's science teachers and astronomy majors, though you will catch the in-house experts depending on what time you stop in. These are passionate people, so come armed with all the questions you've ever had about the stars, and prepare for the answers to blow your mind.

The observatory is open til 9pm, so you'll still be able to get a peek at the planets during those late sunsets of summer, and come winter you can enthrall yourself with the beauty of the cosmos for hours.

Visit on Fridays for safe sun gazing events during the summer.

Address 601 Light Street, Baltimore, MD 21230, +1 (410)685-5225, www.mdsci.org | **Hours** Mon–Fri 10am–5pm | **Tip** Head down to the south side of the Inner Harbor to Baltimore Beach (300 Key Highway, Baltimore, MD 21230, www.baltimorebeach.com) for some urban fun in the sun on one of the seven public beach-volleyball courts built by the city. For locals there are lessons and leagues; for visitors, there are drop-in games.

73 Orchard Street Church
Passageway to freedom

During the abhorrent years of slavery, Baltimore was a divided city. It was a legal practice: many affluent families were slave owners, slave ships docked in the harbor, slave markets existed on Pratt street where thousands of human beings were imprisoned, bought, and sold. At the same time, Baltimore was a haven for free blacks, having the largest population of any city, North or South. The neighborhoods of Sharp-Ledenhall and Seton Hill were tight-knit communities of former slaves, freeborn children, and refugees from the West Indies.

The Underground Railroad was a vast network that helped slaves from the Deep South escape to the free states of the North. Beginning in Georgia and passing up through the Carolinas and Virginia, the route headed to Baltimore, an important stop before the last leg. While on the run, slaves had to be hidden in safe houses and hidden chambers, travelling through swamps and back roads to escape detection. In Baltimore, African Americans wandered the streets as freely as whites, meaning that it was easier to blend in and rest a bit before making the final push into the free state of Pennsylvania.

Orchard Street Church was founded in 1775 by a freed slave, and its first formal home was built in 1825 by the volunteer labor of free blacks and slaves. Additions were built over the decades to accommodate the growing population. By 1882 a full rebuild was carried out by men of color. By this time, though, they were all free.

Rumors of its possible role in Harriet Tubman's Underground Railroad persisted for years but remained unverified. During a restoration in 1992, an underground tunnel was discovered, very close to Austin Woolfolk's slave market on the corner of Pratt and Fremont Streets. The tunnel led north to a portion of railroad tracks and the old Mount Royal Station, where trains would be slowly making their way north.

Address 510–512 Orchard Street, Baltimore, MD 21201, +1 (410)523-8150,
www.gbul.org/orchard-st-church.html | **Hours** Mon–Fri 9am–5pm; call for tours and
church services times | **Tip** The namesake of the neighborhood, St. Elizabeth Ann Seton,
lived in a house on the grounds of St. Mary's Seminary, in which she opened a school for
young children (5400 Roland Avenue, Baltimore, MD 21210, www.stmarys.edu). This place
is now recognized as the birthplace of the Catholic School system in America.
Seton became the first American saint.

74 Ouija 7-Eleven
Parlour games with the dearly departed

The planchette is a mystical tool used to communicate with the spirit world. A small, triangle shaped device, it was attached to a pen and sat on small wheels which, when lightly touched by a spiritual medium, would glide over a paper covered table, writing out messages from the dearly departed. While a popular activity in the seance-crazy Victorian age, the writing was often hard to decipher, leading spiritualists to etch the letters of the alphabet directly into the table. In the 1880s, small homemade boards began popping up for sale in stores specializing in the otherworldly. A clever man from Baltimore had the idea to capitalize on this Victorian obsession with the paranormal and transform this item of mysticism into a mass-produced parlor game. The name he – or should I say, the spirits – gave to his invention eventually became synonymous with the practice itself: Ouija.

In 1890, three people would assemble in a boarding house known as the Lanham Hotel in Mount Vernon. Elijah Bond, the man who would file the patent, Charles Kennard, the man who would manufacture it, and Helen Peters, a powerful medium who would not only assure the inventors that their creation worked, but later the US Patent Office. They asked the spirits what the board should be named, to which it replied "Ouija." Popular lore says it is a combination of the French and German words for "yes," but later research by Ouija enthusiasts found correspondence from Kennard claiming the spirits said it was an ancient Egyptian word meaning "good luck."

The Lanham hotel closed ages ago, and today it's an unremarkable apartment building with a 7-Eleven on the ground floor. In 2015, the city placed a plaque inside the convenience store. Elijah Bond is buried in Greenmount Cemetery, and his previously unmarked grave is now adorned with a headstone emblazoned with – what else – a Ouija board.

Address 529 N Charles Street, Baltimore, MD 21201 | Hours Open 24 hours | Tip Before Baltimore became a hotbed of contemporary art of its own, there was C. Grimaldis Gallery, the city's first gallery devoted to the genre, that's been selling masterpieces and launching major artists' careers since 1977 (523 N Charles Street, Baltimore, MD 21201, www.cgrimaldisgallery.com).

75__Our Playground

Free-range kids in a playground wonderland

Before Camden Yards, before M&T, generations of Baltimore sports fans flocked to Memorial Stadium to watch Orioles baseball and Colts football. The Colts skipped town in dramatic fashion in 1983, and the Orioles needed an upgraded stadium closer to downtown. Memorial had been the centerpiece of the Waverly neighborhood since 1922, and residents were concerned about what would come of the large hole its demolition would leave. Several years of political wrangling, community protests, and local activism led to a solution that likely brings as much joy to the area as the stadium did: Maryland's largest YMCA complex, lush green sports fields, and on the western edge, one of the greatest playgrounds you will likely ever encounter.

Our Playground at Stadium Place is a community affair from top to bottom. Multiple areas feature different themes that stir the senses and encourage the imagination to run wild. There is a puppet theater, swings and jungle gyms, high castle turrets, a rock-climbing wall, tic-tac-toe, and a big xylophone. Large sections are handicapped accessible, so no child is left out, and there's a special gated toddler section so big and little kids can play together safely.

To design the playground, the architect met with 400 children from local elementary schools and asked them for ideas and drawings. The children and their families also were integral in raising $250,000 for their dream park, built by volunteers with recycled building materials.

It's obvious by this point that Our Playground is a very special place, but its story manages to get even more remarkable, and unbelievably heartwarming. In October of 2008 vandals burned the park to the ground. While the community was devastated, they were not deterred. More funds were raised, and the following May the playground was rebuilt, entirely by volunteers, in five days.

Address 900 E 33rd Street, Baltimore, MD 21218, +1 (410)889-9622, www.stadiumplayground.org | Hours Daily dusk–dawn | Tip The 32nd Street Farmers Market in Waverly (400 E 32nd Street, Baltimore, MD 21218, www.32ndstreetmarket.org) is the only one to run year round. Do not miss anything that Blacksauce Kitchen is serving, and do not be dismayed by the line. They're more than worth it.

76__ The Owl Bar

Hoooo's watching?

Its speakeasy days may be ancient history, but for a grandiose bar situated in what was once one of America's most glamorous hotels, the Owl Bar still feels like a secret hideout. The Hotel Belvedere was built in 1903 as the foremost luxury hotel in Baltimore, and as befitting a city of new money trying to make a splash, no expense was spared. It was the place to see and be seen for the local moneyed class. After all, the very point of building such a glamorous hotel was to attract the rich and powerful from across the globe: captains of industry like John D Rockefeller, movie stars like Rudolph Valentino, and the city's own direct (and controversial) connection to royalty, the Duke of Windsor and his gay divorcée wife, Wallis Simpson.

Its first seventeen years saw it as a typical hotel bar, aptly named The Bar Room, a gentlemen-only establishment where the language was coarse and the air thick with cigar smoke. When Prohibition was enacted, there were no intentions to shutter the bar – after all, they were known to throw the best party in Baltimore. So how do you keep the booze flowing when you're already on the radar? You hide in plain sight. Women were granted access, as it was now just a typical humdrum restaurant called The Owl. As is usually the case with rebranding, there were few aesthetic tweaks that added more than ambiance. The name came from the large owl sculptures that were placed over the cash register. To the untrained eye, they were the namesakes. To those in the know they were a signal system: their eyes would glow red when there was whiskey in the basement. In addition, stained-glass panels were installed that told an old nursery rhyme – innocent words that now had a deeper meaning:

A wise old owl sat in an oak

The more he saw the less he spoke

The less he spoke the more he heard

Why can't we be like that wise old bird?

Address 1 E Chase Street, Baltimore, MD 21202, +1 (410)347-0888, www.theowlbar.com | Hours Mon 11:30am–10pm, Tue & Wed 11:30am–midnight, Thu & Fri 11:30am–2am, Sat 11am–2am, Sun 11am–10pm | Tip Don't just drink like a VIP of yesteryear – eat like one too at The Prime Rib (1101 N Calvert Street, Baltimore, MD 21202, www.theprimerib.com), Baltimore's finest steakhouse. Designed to evoke the old-school Hollywood glamour of 1940s supper clubs, it's been the place to go since opening day in 1965.

77 — Painted Screens

Happy little trees in Highlandtown

While driving around the streets of Highlandtown, you might spy a Baltimore tradition that's as ingenious as it is charming. Painted window screens transform the humdrum windows of rowhomes and mom-&-pop businesses into fantastic displays of folk art. It's also practical: you can see out, but no one can see in.

It is believed the first painted screen was done by a Czech immigrant named William Oktavec, who owned a corner grocery store in Northeast Baltimore. During the particularly hot summer of 1913, well before air conditioning, he faced a conundrum. He couldn't sell his produce outside, as the intense heat was making them wilt, and he couldn't keep his doors open to bring in customers and keep things cools, lest flies and other critters get inside. His solution was to paint his window and door screens with images of what he sold inside.

A neighbor admired the genius of opening the house to fresh air all summer while preserving her privacy, and asked Oktavec to paint a colorful scene on her living room window screen. Soon every person on the block wanted one for every window, and Oktavec found himself with a new business.

Oktavec opened an art studio where he sold many of his own works of art and taught classes on his special technique. The most popular scene, which has been reproduced by generations of artists, is a pastoral landscape featuring a red-roofed cottage. The popularity of this particular screen was likely in response to the layout of Highlandtown: the houses don't have lawns, and there are very few trees or other sights of greenery. A country scene is the perfect remedy.

It's a nice surprise cruising the streets and stumbling onto folk art. But if you'd like to take some time to enjoy the genre outside of driving around in a car, the AVAM has many screens by some of the city's most famous local artists on permanent display.

Address Highlandtown, Baltimore, MD 21224 | Hours Viewable from the outside only |
Tip Want a painted screen all your own? Visit Tom Matarazzo at his shop RAZZO
(911 W 36th Street, Baltimore, MD 21211, www.razzoshop.com) in Hampden, where you
can not only bring home the screen of your dreams, but one of his dozens of hand-painted
Christmas ornaments made out of discarded blue crab shells.

78__Peabody Conservatory
Free performance by musical geniuses

The Baltimore Symphony Orchestra is one of the finest in the world: they've been packing houses since 1916, and received tremendous critical acclaim for their discography, including multiple Grammy awards. In 2007 they made musical history, becoming the only major American orchestra to hand the conductor's baton to a woman, the formidable Marin Alsop. She's considered one of the best maestras in the entire world. If classical music was rock 'n' roll, Alsop would be Janis Joplin.

Regular trips to see the BSO perform can be pricy. Fortunately, regular access to extraordinary classical music doesn't have to be. Baltimore attracts some of the most gifted musicians from across the world to come here to study at the institution where Alsop also directs the Graduate Conducting Department at the Peabody Conservatory. Not only does this institution predate the BSO, it's the oldest musical conservatory in the United States, responsible for many of the greatest musicians to ever grace the stage: Pulitzer Prize-winning composer Dominick Argento, Grammy-winning violist Kim Kashkashian, and legendary singer-songwriter Tori Amos who holds the distinction of being the youngest person ever admitted to the Peabody at the tender age of five.

At the Peabody, or the Walters Art Museum next door, you'll see the classical stars of tomorrow performing alongside their professors and mentors, all of whom (like their students) are the best talent the industry has to offer. Best of all? The tickets to these performances are *free*. Through the year the Peabody presents over 100 major concerts and performances: jazz, symphonic, chamber, dance. There's even more culture beyond that, with master classes and lectures being given by some of the world's most extraordinary talent. And, a few times a year, you'll find Marin Alsop herself on stage, baton in hand, guiding the next generation of artists to greatness.

Address 1 E Mount Vernon Place, Baltimore, MD 21202, +1 (410)234-4500, www.peabody.jhu.edu/events | **Hours** Check website for performance and event schedule | **Tip** When the string section needs outfitting they head to Perrin & Associates Violins, an intimate shop where experts can help you select historic instruments that are restored by skilled craftsmen (517 N Charles Street, Baltimore, MD 21201, www.perrinviolins.com).

79__Pink Flamingos Corner

Filthy and fabulous

John Waters is the Patron Saint of Baltimore. A thin and handsome gentleman with a signature pencil-thin moustache, Waters was doing just about everything before any of it was considered "cool." He was out and proud back when Hollywood was forcing people into the celluloid closet. He had Ricki Lake shimmying and shaking on camera in *Hairspray* decades before the words "body positivity" were spoken. And long before RuPaul ever served fish, Waters was serving us Divine, the fiercest drag queen to ever grace the silver screen.

Harris Glenn Milstead was born to a conservative, Baptist, working-class Baltimore family. He was an effeminate boy who discovered he was queer at the age of 17 in a psychiatrist's office. His parents, though reluctant, helped financially support young Glenn as he found himself in the counterculture of the 1960s, where he began dressing in drag. He soon found himself with a second family of self-proclaimed weirdos. It was Waters who gave him the name Divine, with the tagline, "The most beautiful woman in the world… almost".

They had chemistry. Waters wanted to be a filmmaker, but was more captivated with movies from the grindhouse than the arthouse. He left NYU Film School for the familiar sleazy streets of Baltimore, assembled his team of misfits, and got to shooting. They began to build a reputation for gritty shorts before moving into feature films. A desire to outdo himself and film "an exercise in bad taste" led to *Pink Flamingos*, the cult-classic movie about the "filthiest person alive," played by none other than Divine herself. Pay respects to her memory on this street corner that was the setting for the most infamous moment in a film that featured cannibalism, incest, sodomy, masturbation, and more utterly revolting acts: the completely non-faked moment when Divine eats *[Spoiler Alert]* dog poop.

Address W Read Street & Tyson Street, Baltimore, MD 21201 | Hours Unrestricted |
Tip The Arena Players is the oldest continually operating African-American community
theater in the country. Don't be put off by the "amateur" status: there's not a single show that
won't have you on your feet by curtain call (801 McCulloh Street, Baltimore, MD 21201,
+1 (410)728-6500, www.arenaplayersinc.com).

80__Pool No. 2

Swimming during segregation

It is not surprising that much of the evidence of legal segregation in the US has been destroyed, although this despicable practice was only outlawed nationally in 1964. There is a secret spot in Druid Hill Park where a relic of these times has been transformed by artist and Baltimore native Joyce J. Scott into a piece of art that simultaneously honors the struggles of the community and celebrates the joy they experienced on hot summer days at "Negroe Pool No. 2."

In 1953, the NAACP successfully forced City Hall to desegregate the municipal pool system. On opening day, over 100 African Americans swam in Druid Hill's Pool No. 1, originally "whites only"; one white person braved the waters of Pool No. 2. The next year, Baltimore decided to close Pool No. 2 but never demolished it. The abandoned pool sat empty and fenced off for 40 years until the city decided to repurpose the land. A survey of local residents showed that many held onto cherished memories of the pool. So it was preserved and repurposed through art into a place of reflection and community building.

Today's Druid Hill Park Pool No. 2 is easy to miss from the street. Four modernist columns are meant to evoke the outline of the original ticket house. The red and orange swirled concrete patterns in the sidewalk – based on traditional African patterns representing tranquillity and peace – lead to a flight of descending marble stairs. From here you can see the roof of the former men's dressing room, with a mosaic of undulating blue tiles representing water. The pool itself has been filled with soil and is now a lush island of grass, surrounded by the original pool equipment: ladders, lifeguard station, diving board.

Joyce J. Scott is considered one of the most brilliant African-American artists of modern times. In 2016, she was awarded a Genius Grant from the MacArthur Fellows Program.

Address 800 Wyman Park Drive, Baltimore, MD 21211, +1 (410)396-3838 | **Hours** Daily dawn–dusk | **Tip** Being one of the city's favorite daughters, Joyce Scott's breathtaking work can be seen up close and personal at the Baltimore Museum of Art (10 Art Museum Drive, Baltimore, MD 21218, www.artbma.org), one of many museums where her pieces are part of the permanent collection.

81__Pratt Street

First blood of the Civil War

Everyone who made it through American History class knows that the Civil War effectively began at Fort Sumter in South Carolina. After the state seceded in 1860, the US Army attacked the garrison, and the line between the sides was officially drawn. What isn't mentioned in that history lesson is the fact that there were no casualties in that attack. It would be another week for the first blood to spill, which it did on Pratt Street, in the tourist district on the north side of the Inner Harbor.

Before it was lined with fancy hotels and chain restaurants, Pratt Street was the main thoroughfare between the city's two most important railroad stations: Penn Station which served trains to the North, and Camden Yards which dispatched trains to the South. After declaring war, President Lincoln called for 75,000 volunteer soldiers from the North to travel to the South to quell the insurrection. On April 19th, troops from the 6th Massachusetts Regiment arrived at Penn Station and boarded horse-drawn carriages to Camden Yards to continue their journey. Maryland was a border state where slavery was still legal, with many sympathetic towards the Confederacy. Those sympathizers intended to show the troops that Baltimore held the nickname of "Mobtown" for a reason.

First, the mob created a roadblock on Pratt Street, forcing the troops to abandon their carriages and continue on foot. The mob followed, then surrounded them. They began to throw bricks and stones at the soldiers, which caused the Union troops to respond in kind with bullets. The altercation quickly escalated into a full-scale riot, with the soldiers continuing to march towards Camden Yards, defending themselves as necessary against civilian attacks. By the time they boarded the train, four soldiers and twelve rioters had been killed. Visit 337 E Hamburg (see ch. 3) to learn about subsequent events.

Address Begin at the old President Street Station (601 S President Street, Baltimore, MD 21202). Head north to Pratt Street, turn left, and continue walking west to retrace the soldiers' path. Turn left again on South Eutaw Street and walk one block south to arrive at the former Camden Yards Station. | **Hours** Unrestricted | **Tip** Home of the last surviving and only Catholic signer of the Declaration of Independence, the 1811 urban mansion of John Carroll is open for tours. Fabulously opulent by standards both today and yesterday, this mansion was called "the finest home in Baltimore" for many years (800 E Lombard Street, Baltimore, MD 21202, www.carrollmuseums.org).

82 __ The QG

Puttin' on the ritz

Walking amidst the grandiose buildings of Downtown, you can't help but wonder what Baltimore was like during its heyday when titans of industry walked its streets. While the booming days of railroads and robber barons may be a thing of the past, there is still a place where a dapper gent can feel at home: the QG department store on the corner of Lombard and Calvert.

Founder Craig Martin opened the Quintessential Gentleman as a barbershop to fulfill a personal need. Exceptional service and luxurious surroundings were common for salons catering to a female clientele – why not create a similar experience for men? Martin wanted a space where a man could get a straight-razor shave or a proper beard shaping, and experience the lost art of the old-time full barber facial. The QG grew from a four-chair storefront into a five-story building devoted to the finer things in life.

First came a spa for massages and expanded grooming services. Once a man looks good, he needs a place to go, so a private cigar club (complete with smoking jackets) was added. When another floor in the building became available, Martin opened a tailoring shop where men could have custom suits made, and it grew into an entire floor of read-to-wear fashion. The QG has since taken over the entire building, adding a speakeasy, a members-only restaurant, and a private clubhouse complete with golf simulator. They've even added a fashion boutique to serve some of the most ardent customers at the tailoring shop: women.

While a club, the QG is not closed off to visitors passing through town. Block off a few hours and treat yourself to a straight-razor shave, order your first custom suit, drink a Prohibition-style cocktail, or play a round at Pebble Beach indoors. It's very hard to argue with their philosophy: You've worked hard to get where you are, so treat yourself to the QG life. You've earned it.

Address 31 S Calvert Street, Baltimore, MD 21202, +1 (410)685-7428, www.theqg.com | Hours Mon 11:30am–8pm, Tue–Fri 10am–8pm, Sat 9am–5pm, Sun 11am–5pm | Tip If you're looking for a place to recharge, park yourself at the Bun Shop (22 Light Street, Baltimore, MD 21202), where you'll find one of the city's best cups of coffee, as well as their signature (delicious) stuffed buns, which make for a perfect afternoon snack.

83 _ Rachael's Dowry B&B

George Washington slept here

Living up to its name, Ridgely's Delight is one of the smallest, most charming neighborhoods in Baltimore, filled with tiny houses that line quiet streets, quite the contrast to the boisterous crowds that fill the adjacent roads come gameday. In the middle of this quaint historic district you'll find one of old Baltimore's most beautiful homes: an 8,000-square-foot mansion built in 1798 that's now a B&B: Rachael's Dowry.

There is no one here named Rachael, nor did Rachael ever live here. The name comes from the origins of the neighborhood itself, as every house in the area stands on lands that were gifted to Colonel Charles Ridgely on his wedding day in 1667 by the father of his beautiful bride, Rachael Howard (the original "Ridgely's Delight"). The mansion was built over a century later by a wealthy politician named Michael Warner, who was a close friend of George and Martha Washington. Shortly before his death, Washington was on his way from Baltimore to Alexandria when he was hurt in a carriage accident, and asked to be brought to the house for doctors to tend to him. A statue of Washington with his arm in a sling stood in the yard until 1972, when it was purchased by an antiques dealer. The street the house sits on now bears his name.

After Washington's statue left, the house fell on hard times, and was completely uninhabitable until 2007 when renovations began to restore it to its former glory. It now stands as a portal to another time, furnished entirely with antiques and faithful reproductions from the Federal, Victorian, and Arts and Crafts periods, and a library outfitted with original Duncan Phyfe furniture. There are countless beautiful touches that catch the eye, but one of the most special can be found right beneath your feet: the original tongue-and-groove hardwood flooring which once upon a time hosted the aching feet of the father of our country.

Address 637 Washington Boulevard, Baltimore, MD 21230, +1 (410)752-0805, www.rachaelsdowrybedandbreakfast.com | **Hours** By appointment only | **Tip** Some of the best food in the city isn't coming out of the much-lauded restaurant scene, but rather from a small shop called Culinary Architecture: a gourmet grocery with superlative prepared foods and baked goods. Though mostly carry out, ask if their "secret garden" is open because it's a lovely place to rest your legs (767 Washington Boulevard, Baltimore, MD 21230, www.culinaryarchitecture.com).

84 Riverside Avenue

Charm City's charming row houses

Early cities were cramped, crowded places before the horseless carriage or the electric trolley, when people lived as close as they could to wherever the jobs were. Eventually, the more affluent moved to greener spaces and larger homes, leaving cities to the working classes who couldn't afford the elbow room. The suburbs grew and grew, from the early days of stately Victorians through the age of McMansions. Now, however, people are getting back to basics, embracing minimalism with the tiny-house movement. If you're looking for one of your own, you need not seek out a parcel of land or a flatbed trailer to build upon – Baltimore's been in the tiny-house business for centuries.

The signature residential style in Charm City is the row house, like a townhouse, but more compact. Wherever you found industry – the docks of Fell's Point, the rail yards of Pigtown, the factories of Locust Point, the mills of Remington – you found row houses. They began being built en masse when the population of Baltimore doubled in 1790–1800 as business started to boom. To keep up with the demand for laborers, rural slave owners rented slaves to urban businessmen, and in a densely populated city they were permitted to live in their own dwellings in extremely tight quarters.

Two of the last surviving examples of this style of homes are 1124 and 1126 Riverside Avenue. Each is one-and-a-half stories with a single door and window located on the first floor, a pitched gable roof with dormer window framing out the half-story. These were bare-bones dwellings built decades before public utilities: water was brought in from wells down the road, chamber pots were used for waste, heat was provided by a small fireplace that also allowed for meager cooking. They were eventually combined into a single home which, prior to later additions, gave the owners close to 400 square feet of living space.

Address 1124–1126 Riverside Avenue, Baltimore, MD 21230 | Hours Unrestricted | Tip The houses in Federal Hill command a pretty penny thanks to their historic charm, even if they're not exactly spacious. Consider 200 ½ E Montgomery Street: this private residence is only 9 feet wide, making it the narrowest house in Baltimore (200 ½ E Montgomery Street, Baltimore, MD 21230).

85 — Roland Park Shopping Center

A strip mall with charm

In the unlikely event that you've managed to avoid the allure of wandering around a mall shopping for the newest fashion and the best sales, you've most certainly driven past the tens of thousands that line America's suburban roadways and for that, you have Baltimore to thank. The concept of the suburb dates back to the late 19th century, when the Industrial Revolution caused major cities to become congested, polluted, and all but unlivable. Baltimore in particular saw its population triple from 1820 to 1860.

While moving outside the city limits would seem like a logical solution, primitive transportation systems and a lack of formal infrastructure made it nearly impossible for anyone who was not obscenely wealthy. The invention of the electric street car changed everything. In 1885, English inventor Leo Daft developed a compound rail for electric railways, and the first American installation of this technology was the conversion of the Baltimore / Hampden horse-drawn carriage line to the modern system. The city was about to be transformed.

The planned garden suburb of Roland Park was first conceived in 1891, designed to have a pastoral aesthetic that would mimic the English countryside. Its natural boundaries were meant to give it a sense of self-containment and give its residents a feeling of safety from the perceived dangers of the city. Soon afterwards, the age of the automobile began, and affluent Roland Park citizens were some of the few who could afford their hefty price tags. In 1907, the concept of a shopping center was created, and built on the corner of Upland Road and Roland Avenue in the English Tudor style. Set away from the street to allow for another newfangled invention called the "parking lot," it still hosts several storefronts today and an architectural aesthetic that seamlessly blended it into the community.

Address 4800 Roland Avenue, Baltimore, MD 21230 | **Hours** Unrestricted from the outside; see individual shops for hours | **Tip** Chef Cindy Wolf is not only one of Baltimore's best chefs but a national darling, with multiple James Beard nominations for best chef in the Mid Atlantic. Her Petit Louis Bistro serves traditional French food that's positively dripping old-world charm (4800 Roland Avenue, Baltimore, MD 21210, www.petitlouis.com).

86__Royal Farms

Winner, winner, chicken dinner

It is only natural that you would Google "best food in Baltimore" if you're coming for a visit or just seeking a great meal. You'll likely seek out a quality crabcake, and you may be swayed into an elegant farm-to-table dinner at one of the city's many excellent restaurants. But if you *really* want to eat the way Baltimoreans eat, you want a "chicken box" – deep-fried chicken with a side of fries.

There are a few local chains that do a fine job of satiating the appetite – Hip Hop Fried Chicken comes to mind – but if you're seeking a fried chicken that is so transcendent that you would gladly take it over a four-star meal any day of the week, you're going to have to look in a place you'd never expect to have such a stellar meal.

Royal Farms is not a restaurant, but a chain of convenience stores and gas stations. Inside each impeccably clean location you will find the usual suspects for such an establishment: chips, cigarettes, motor oil, coffee, cell phone accessories, processed meat sticks. You won't be able to miss the hot-food counter, and you won't be able to resist the smell. Most fast-food joints fry up frozen breaded chicken, but not here: every piece is fresh and breaded by hand on site and then pressure fried to create a golden crispy crust that's not greasy, locking in tender, succulent meat which is likely the juiciest you'll ever find (and most definitely the best you'll ever find at a convenience store and gas station).

The fries don't come out of a bag in the freezer, either. Royal Farms serves an uncommon East Coast specialty known as "Western fries": potatoes that are hand cut into thick wedges, then tossed lightly in a highly seasoned batter, and deep fried. The result is something that tastes like a hybrid of a French fry and baked potato, and pairs perfectly with Chesapeake sauce, a blend of two local favorites, Old Bay and Duke's Mayo.

Address 1530 Russell Street, Baltimore, MD 21230, +1 (410)962-0414, www.royalfarms.com |
Hours Open 24/7 | Tip Of the many Royal Farms locations, the finest might be across the
street from the Horseshoe Casino, which provides for excellent people watching, as well as high
rolling (1525 Russell Street, Baltimore, MD 21230, www.caesars.com/horseshoe-baltimore).

87 __ Schuler School For The Arts

Draw me like one of your French girls

Baltimore is a city of juxtaposed views – handsome old buildings adjacent to glistening contemporary developments, bubbling streams under roaring highways, stately public monuments overshadowed by loud modernist artworks. With cutting edge institutions like MICA and the AVAM, you'd be forgiven if you thought that the artistic ethos here was exclusively one of constant forward momentum. The truth is that art is studied and created in both directions – with some breaking boundaries towards the future, and others turning towards the past, intensely studying the realism and techniques of the old masters in a small townhome just blocks from the Washington Monument: the Schuler School for the Arts.

Hans Schuler was a renowned early 20th-century sculptor who created public monuments, memorials, and busts. His son, also a sculptor, opened it as a school in 1959. It has remained in the family as a highly competitive and very intimate institution of learning. The study of the classics is an intense process, where creativity is equally matched by the sciences. Anatomy is studied in detail, so the eye can be trained to dissect the human body into the structures of muscle and bone. Mathematics plays a pivotal role as students are taught how to measure precisely and scale their subjects, how to compose in ratios, and how to understand angles so that light and shadow can be naturally conveyed. Even the mediums used are fashioned as they were centuries ago: statues are molded and cast by hand, canvases are stretched, pigments are ground and blended into oil to create paint. There are no majors: each student must study portrait, still-life, and landscape painting, sculpture, and drawing.

Schuler opens its doors several times a year for exhibitions, but can also be viewed privately (and sometimes in action) by appointment.

Address 7 E Lafayette Avenue, Baltimore, MD 21202, +1 (410)685-3568, www.schulerschool.com | Hours Check website for current information on classes and events | Tip One of Schuler's greatest works can be found in Baltimore's greatest park: the General Casimir Pulaski Monument in Patterson Park (2806 Eastern Avenue, Baltimore, MD 21224, www.pattersonpark.com), paid for nearly entirely by small donations by members of the city's Polish community.

88 _Second Chance Architectural Salvage

Baltimore's biggest treasure chest

Baltimore's shopping scene circles around local artisans and vintage stores, making each day out a treasure hunt with one-in-a-million finds. You'll want to make your way down to Pigtown for 200,000 square feet of some of the most remarkable items you'll find anywhere: Second Chance Architectural Salvage.

Their inventory is salvaged from properties before they are renovated, so the items here are positively remarkable, not to mention so affordable you won't believe they're accurate. If you're looking for a way to outfit your pad, you'll find row upon row of couches, chairs, and tables from different design periods. The inventory is constantly changing, so it's worth repeat visits.

Seeking something a bit quirkier? Second Chance has an entire section of church pews and stained-glass windows, another section of antique pre-1960s appliances, and a room full of priceless antiques for a fraction of the price you'll find elsewhere (in fact, this is where a lot of antique shops in Washington, DC and New York City find their inventory). You'll often find yourself surprised by items that are so niche and retro that they'll bring back tons of memories, like vintage jukeboxes and cigarette machines, 1950s televisions, and home bars from the 1970s made from tufted leather with a mirrored countertop.

Not only will you feel good walking away with the deal of the century, but Second Chance is a non-profit organization that was formed to help create jobs for individuals who have had difficulty finding employment. They have a workforce development program that has trained hundreds of women and men. Every piece they sell stays out of a landfill (thus far, over 2 million pounds worth!). In more ways than one, Second Chance delivers on its name.

Address 1700 Ridgely Street, Baltimore, MD 21230, +1 (410)385-1700, www.secondchanceinc.org | **Hours** Daily 9am−5pm | **Tip** On Pigtown's main street, Washington Boulevard, is the 9/10 Condition Sneaker Boutique, a shop that sells lit sneakers on consignment, as well as vintage streetwear and pop-culture items from the 80s and 90s. Of note: the sizeable collection of Michael Jordan memorabilia (775 Washington Boulevard, Baltimore, MD 21230).

89 __ Senator Theater
Movie premier glamour meets high tech

At night, when the Senator Theater lights up its marquee in all its art-deco neon glory, it looks like something out of an idyllic Hollywood dreamscape. Many filmmakers agree, which is why it may seem familiar; you may have spotted it in several of the films made by local boys John Waters and Barry Levinson, both of whom hold their red-carpet premieres here. One of its most legendary appearances was in the neo-noir science-fiction classic, *12 Monkeys*, where it was the venue for an Alfred Hitchcock retrospective that doubled as a hiding place for Bruce Willis and Madeleine Stowe.

While the suburban multiplexes have stepped up the movie going experience with features such as recliners, cocktail bars, and in-seat dining, the humble 1930's Senator is still *the* place to see a film in Baltimore. It has the classic accents of a vintage theater – elaborate murals, private balcony boxes, and a giant gold curtain over its 40-foot screen. It also has all the technical bells and whistles it needs to provide a top-notch movie-going experience.

In fact, the Senator was selected to be the first venue to participate in the Historic Cinema Certification Program, created by George Lucas' THX to upgrade classic movie theaters with state-of-the-art sound and projection. When a big film premieres, fans flock to the Senator, camping out and forming lines around the block, and news crews follow (so if you've ever wanted to get on TV in your Jar Jar Binks costume, this is the place to be). The National Trust for Historic Preservation calls it "America's quintessential independent movie house."

The sidewalk out front acts as a small monument to Baltimore's film history, in the style of Grauman's Chinese Theater in LA. You'll find the celebrities' handprints and signatures permanently etched in the concrete, as well as plaques honoring films and television series that prominently feature the city of Baltimore.

Address 5904 York Road, Baltimore, MD 21212, +1 (410)323-4424, www.thesenatortheatre.com | **Hours** Check website for current movie schedule | **Tip** Any visit to the Senator must be paired with a visit to Amazing Spiral (5851 York Road, Baltimore, MD 21212, www.amazingspiral.com), a shop specializing in books, comics, games, and community. There are clubs for multiple fandoms that meet every week, an arts and crafts center for the kids, and tons of friendly folks both behind and in front of the counter that make it more of a second home than a simple comic-book store.

90 Sharp Street Church
Birth of a movement

Sharp Street United Methodist Church cuts an imposing figure in contrast to the row homes and parking lots that surround it – appropriate for one of the most important Black churches in our nation's history. It's current structure was built in 1898, but the congregation itself dates back to 1787, when free people of color left the Lovely Lane Methodist Church (see ch. 58) due to its segregation policy, an odd fact, since the Methodist Movement was staunchly anti-slavery. The community held services in their own homes, forming the Colored Methodist Society. Soon, free and enslaved Black people made up over 20% of all American Methodists.

They at last acquired a building of their own in 1802 in Downtown Baltimore, the first church building owned by African Americans. A bustling community hub, it became a central location for the discussion of abolitionism, activism, and African colonization. Famed abolitionist Frederick Douglass was a member of the congregation and sang in the church choir. In the 1860s they founded the Centenary Bible Institute, which grew into another Baltimore landmark, Morgan State University.

In 1898, the congregation built a grand neo-Gothic church on Dolphin Street. The *Baltimore Sun* called it "the handsomest church for a colored congregation in the state." In this new building, history would seemingly repeat itself.

Like Frederick Douglass before her, Lillie Mae Carroll Jackson sang in the Sharp Street Church choir as a child. The church hosted meetings of the Niagara Movement and the civil-rights groups that would lead to the development of the NAACP. She organized the Baltimore chapter of the NAACP in 1935, serving as its president until 1970 and becoming known as "the Mother of the Civil Rights Movement." When she died in 1975, Sharp Street held a funeral service for her with over 1,200 in attendance.

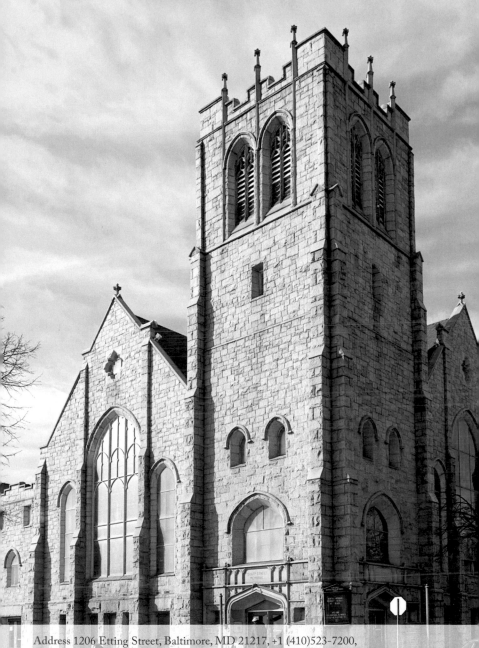

Address 1206 Etting Street, Baltimore, MD 21217, +1 (410)523-7200, www.sharpstreet.org | Hours Sun Services 10am; call for visiting hours | Tip Jackson's townhouse was purchased by Morgan State University, one of America's historically black colleges, and turned into the Lillie Mae Carroll Jackson Museum that tells the story of the Civil Rights Movement, with a focus on Baltimore history (1320 Eutaw Place, Baltimore, MD 21217, www.explorebaltimore.org).

91 Society of Model Engineers

They choo-choo-choose you

Ever since the first track was laid nearly 200 years ago, children of all ages have been obsessed with trains: from the first Lionel locomotive to Thomas the Tank Engine. In the city that started it all, some kids never stopped playing with trains.

The Baltimore Society of Model Engineers got its start in 1932 with a simple magazine ad, which brought ten good men to the home of a Mr. George Nixon. These enthusiasts spent their first few years bouncing between each others homes, helping each other build models, swapping tips and tricks, until one day it was decided they needed a space all their own. They built permanent displays in three different homes before they finally came to settle in their current location in 1952 and have been building upon their original masterwork ever since.

The model is nothing short of a masterpiece. Visitors can expect to see all sorts of locomotives – steam, diesel, electric – in both O and HO scales (the engineers will happily explain all about the differences!). The trains run through 1,560 square feet of hand-built model landscapes, bucolic pastoral scenes, idyllic small towns, and faithful reproductions of ornate Baltimore landmarks like the Bromo Seltzer Tower. Not an inch of the model was made in haste – look for "hidden" details such as the workers inside the coal mine, the Depression-era hobo camp under the HO bridge, the spot-on interior of the old-time soda shop, and the finer details of the city buildings where you can see people relaxing in their apartments or participating in a little household DIY.

The most delightful attraction might be the railroaders themselves, who keep volunteer hours at the society to show the public around and get a brand new generation as excited about the Society as they were when they were children. They might just inspire you to feel like a kid again yourself.

Address 225 W Saratoga Street, Baltimore, MD 21201, +1 (410)837-2763, www.modelengineers.com | Hours Sat 7pm–11pm, Sun 1pm–5pm | Tip For all your spiritual and supernatural needs, check out Grandma's Candle Shop, which carries items dear to all religions and beliefs. They've got everything from healing crystals to voodoo dolls, and they give advice for all sorts of mysticism (227 W Saratoga Street, Baltimore, MD 21201, +1 (410)685-4289, www.grandmascandleshop.com/info.html).

92 The Sound Garden
Birthplace of Record Store Day

Logically, vinyl records should have gone the way of the 8-track, and yet are still here. Vinyl sales have been steadily rising, thanks to a new generation of audiophiles who find both the sound and ritual of records to be unmatched by any newer technology. While vinyl has been able to survive despite perpetual modernization, the independent music store has not. The local record store was a gathering place, where people made friends, discovered new artists, and could spend countless hours sharing their passion. On a fateful night at The Sound Garden in Fell's Point, an idea was hatched that would change the music business forever.

Record-store owners worldwide knew they were in trouble. A late night brainstorming session at Sound Garden gave birth to the idea of Record Store Day, an annual celebration that's been held every April since 2007. Each participating store would throw an all-day party with once-in-a-lifetime opportunities for music fans: limited edition record releases, in-store performances, fan meet and greets – all tailored for each store's personality. It was an instant success, and it gets bigger year after year. Albums and 7" that have had limited pressings and one-day distributions can go for thousands of dollars on the collectors circuit. Celebrations have spread from a few hundred small shops in the US and UK to thousands spanning six continents. For some, Record Store Day is more important than Christmas.

Sound Garden is still a must-visit the other 364 days of the year. Open seven days a week, you can find far more than vinyl here: books, video games, new and used albums on LP and CD, and pop-culture ephemera. Whether you're searching for something specific or looking for a brand new musical discovery, introduce yourself at the counter and let the staff show you why the independent music store is an institution worth saving.

Address 1616 Thames Street, Baltimore, MD 21231, +1 (410)563-9011, www.cdjoint.com |
Hours Daily 10am–10pm | **Tip** You might not be too excited about hot dogs for lunch,
but one trip to Stuggy's Fells Point Hot Dogs (809 S Broadway, Baltimore, MD 21231)
will change that. These are hot dogs turned to 11, with toppings such as gyro meat, fried
jerk chicken, crab mac & cheese, and other eccentric bits of culinary flair that will make you
wonder why you've been settling for just plain old mustard for so long.

93___Stephen Wise Baltimore
Lookin' smart, feelin' fine

With the creative class growing every day, there's no doubt you'll come across a person or two for whom fashion is not just about style: it's the reason for their very existence. In a city this sharp, there's one man who stands head and shoulders above the rest, a man who doesn't follow fashion but defines it: Stephen Wise.

Wise grew up in a family that didn't have a fortune to spend on trendy clothing or expensive name-brand sneakers. He's tall and slender like a model, which made it difficult to find off-the-rack clothing that would fit his frame. Constantly needing his clothes pinned and hemmed was the thing that gave him the inspiration to learn how to sew, but it was an act of fate that gave him style. A fellow parishioner at this family's church owned a formalwear store and gifted Wise designer menswear, the sort of attire that one would associate with a dapper older gentleman rather than a teenager from East Baltimore. Wise was immediately hooked. He got an after-school job working for a local clothing designer, where he learned to sew and make patterns. He attended Howard University and opened a fashionable men's clothing boutique inside his dorm room.

Today Mr. Wise has brought his talents to the historic Lexington Market, operating a store on North Paca Street that's hard to miss: the ever-changing window displays are always eye catchers, often exquisitely tailored suits made of bright, colorful fabrics and unexpected patterns. Inside his fashionable wonderland you'll get to meet the man himself, who can turn you into a walking masterpiece. You'll find pieces, the likes of which you'll never find in a boring, generic shopping-mall store. If you find yourself inspired by what you see, you can sign up for a sewing class with the man himself. But if you *really* want to treat yourself, you'll call ahead and book an appointment for your bespoke suit.

Address 216 N Paca Street, Baltimore, MD 21201, +1 (667)309-6021,
www.lexingtonmarket.com/vendor/stephen-wise | Hours Mon–Sat 8:30am–6pm |
Tip Across the street in Lexington Market you'll find Faidley's (203 N Paca Street, Baltimore,
MD 21201, www.faidleyscrabcakes.com), which makes what is widely believed to be the best
crabcake in the country. While that's a title that Baltimoreans will argue about for the ages,
there's no disputing that this is one of the finest you'll ever have the pleasure of eating.

94 __ Sudbrook Park
Green living in the city

It's likely you've enjoyed Frederick Law Olmstead's work even if you don't know his name. The father of landscape architecture, Olmstead was the visionary behind New York City's Central and Prospect Parks, the White City of the 1893 Chicago World's Fair, and the National Zoo in Washington, DC. A certifiable genius, he sculpted landscapes with an eye to what they would look like in ten, twenty, or even one hundred or more years. His subtle touches are all over Baltimore, from Patterson Park, which he personally designed, to Leakin Park, landscaped by his sons. In the Northeast lies one of his most ambitious concepts: the ideal suburban community. There are only three of these patented Olmstead neighborhoods in America: Riverside in Chicago, Druid Hills in Atlanta, and Baltimore's Sudbrook Park.

After the Chicago World's Fair, Olmstead began conceptualizing a community that would allow people to live with nature yet close to the crowded cities that had been rapidly industrialized in the 19th century. He envisioned a place where winding roads would create a sense of isolation and removal from the filth of the city. Trees were strategically planted, taking their relationship with the sun into account, to create a playfulness with shadow and light. Wide streets and sidewalks were, in the age of horse-drawn carriages, meant to encourage leisurely strolls around the neighborhood. Upon completion, 16 deed restrictions were enacted to ensure the character of Sudbrook would be preserved, and nearly a century later, a designation as a National Historic district further protected the heart of the community.

While there has been development around the edges of the neighborhood, including a controversial subway addition by the Maryland Transit Administration, the heart of the community remains the same, and well preserved by the proud residents of Sudbrook.

Address Sudbrook Lane & Upland Road, Baltimore, MD 21208, www.sudbrookpark.org | Hours Daily dawn–dusk | Tip Four of Olmstead's lesser-known works surround one of Baltimore's most famous icons: the Washington Monument in Mount Vernon (699 Washington Place, Baltimore, MD 21201, www.mvpconservancy.org), the Peabody Library (17 E Mount Vernon Place, Baltimore, MD 21202, www.peabodyevents.library.jhu.edu/about), the Engineers Club (11 W Mount Vernon Place, Baltimore, MD 21201, www.esb.org), and the Walters Art Museum (600 N Charles Street, Baltimore, MD 21201, www.thewalters.org, see ch. 105).

95 Tha Flower Factory

They're bringing nature back

Cities are built over where nature once stood, and just like plants and trees, they grow, they die, they are reborn. Baltimore has been bullish about combating urban blight with things like murals and real-estate incentives – but while they build towards the future, they also are building towards the past. First there were the neighborhood activists who were interested in developing a new model of feeding a city, reclaiming vacant lots and transforming them into miniature farms that would grow produce in the middle of food deserts. Then their numbers grew, and the Farm Alliance of Baltimore was formed. Soon it was hard to argue against this far-flung idea; while many were skeptical how gardening would fare in the inner city, others quickly proved transformative for the communities they sprung up in.

Not all of these farms are for food. Tha Flower Factory, a formerly vacant half-acre lot in the Broadway East neighborhood, is for cut flowers. The brainchild of Walker Marsh, an experienced urban farmhand, its mission is not just to beautify the city, but also to nourish it. Flower farms do more than provide jobs. In many vacant-to-value situations, pollutants that exist in the soil make it unsuitable for growing any sort of food, but flowers are fair game. In fact, flowerbeds can actually transform these lots by drawing contaminants out of the soil, slowly purifying it year after year until it once again becomes suitable for edible vegetation. And when it comes down to economics, selling flowers to local florists generates more money per acre than vegetables do, meaning that Tha Flower Factory may one day be doing much more than beautifying the neighborhood. As these farms and gardens sprout and thrive, so does the vision of many more lots across the city blooming in vibrant color, putting money back into the communities of the people who helped them grow.

Address 1433 N Gay Street, Baltimore, MD 21213, +1 (443)500-8640, www.thaflowerfactory.com | **Hours** Unrestricted | **Tip** Want to help support urban farming? Keep your eye out for the Real Food Farms Mobile Market, a food truck that brings the farmers market to different "food desert" neighborhoods each day (www.realfoodfarm.civicworks.com/get-food/mobile-farmers-market).

96___Thomas A. Dixon Jr. Observation Area

Up, up, and away

Air travel, a feat that human beings spent millennia trying to accomplish, is now something we all take for granted. In fact, most people associate air travel with negative experiences and enervating processes, like security checkpoints, lousy customer service, and cramped spaces when you actually get to your seat. Barely a century ago, however, flight was seen as a marvel of modern technology that was so utterly fantastic, it was practically magic. Certainly it's hard to capture that feeling again at the airport, but a visit to Thomas A. Dixon Jr. Observation Area might rekindle that sense of amazement.

Baltimore Washington International Airport (BWI) is a quick ride south on the Light Rail (not to mention a great airport for securing discount flights for Baltimore or Washington, DC, as it's a hub for many budget carriers who skip DC's more expensive Dulles or National Airports). Walking south down the BWI trail loop, you will come across a scenic 12.5-mile (20-km) trail popular with joggers and bikers, leading to Friendship Park and the Thomas A. Dixon Jr. Observation Area. It looks like any other suburban glen, complete with playground and a picnic area. You'll only realize this is no ordinary park when the ground begins to rumble.

Soon, you will hear the loud roar of a jet engine, which is your cue to look up and keep your eyes on the sky. The Observation Area is less than 700 feet (200 m) past runway L33, so when commercial airplanes pass over, they're so close that you feel as if you could reach straight up and touch them. Watching over one million pounds of metal lift off and soar into the sky is a breathtaking sight, and it will, or it should, remind you of the days when air travel seemed glamorous, exciting – and magical.

Address 1911 Dorsey Road, Glen Burnie, MD 21061, +1 (410)222-7317, www.aacounty.org/locations-and-directions/bwi-trail | **Hours** Daily dawn – dusk | **Tip** The beautiful (seriously) BWI Airport (7050 Friendship Road, Baltimore, MD 21240, www.bwiairport.com/en) isn't as well known as the two larger area airports closer to Washington, DC, which is why it's a major hub for discount airliners, as well as a hub for budget-friendly Southwest Airlines. Inside BWI, look for the most beautiful crab in Maryland: a 500lb, 10-footer made of stained glass.

97 — Tiffany Windows At Brown Memorial Church

Blessed light from the hand of an artist

Louis Comfort Tiffany is one of the greatest artistic geniuses in history. He began as a painter, moved into furniture and textile design, and then became one of the most sought after names in interiors (President Chester A. Arthur refused to move into the White House until Tiffany redecorated it). Then he turned his eye to glass.

Churches have been associated with stained glass since the Middle Ages, as streaming light is considered to be symbolic of the hand of God, and passing it through sanctified windows with images from the Bible transformed it into the light of providence. When word spread about a studio in New York that was producing windows with colored glass, stretched, and textured to create images of awe-inspiring beauty – well, suffice to say there was no church being built in America that didn't desire a very exclusive, and very expensive, Tiffany window. And for Brown Memorial Church in Bolton Hill, only the best would do.

The church was built in 1870 by Isabella Brown, widow of financier and B&O Railroad co-founder George Brown. One of the richest women in the world, she singlehandedly funded the church as a monument to her dearly departed husband. She spared no expense – a soaring vaulted ceiling, ornate Gothic-revival embellishments, 150 hardlined gaslights illuminating the massive space. Commissioning a set of Tiffany windows was a must.

Most of Tiffany's sacred works have been destroyed or removed as midcentury urban flight forced many churches to close. The parishioners of Brown Memorial opted to remain in Baltimore rather than flee to the suburbs. As a result, the newly restored church continues to glow with the light of eleven original handcrafted Tiffany windows – the largest collection in its original setting.

Address 1316 Park Avenue, Baltimore, MD 21217, +1 (410)523-1542, www.browndowntown.org | **Hours** Mon–Fri 9am–3pm; services Sun 11am | **Tip** Can't get enough Tiffany? Grab a cab over to the St. Mark's Lutheran Church (1900 St. Paul Street, Baltimore, MD 21218, www.stmarksbaltimore.org) where Tiffany designed more than just the windows – he designed the church's entire interior.

98__Toilet Bowl Races
Trickling down the avenue

What happens when a child outgrows the quaint competition of the soapbox derby? They become smarter, stronger, more driven, and much more mad. Some other former-children race stock cars or bicycles. In Baltimore, they race toilets.

The annual Toilet Bowl Races had humble origins, as most toilet-related things do. Steve Baker, a local artist, wanted to create a left-of-center fundraiser to help build a local skate park. The park opened several years ago, but the golden flow of thrill seekers continues to careen down the pitched slope of Chestnut Avenue each September during the Hampden Festival. The rules: each racer must be 100% gravity powered and launched by a team of pushers; the race vehicle must have a break and be steerable; and it must include one *clean* defecation device (emphasis theirs, so no one gets any dirty ideas). Teams compete in single elimination races over the course of an afternoon until one team reigns supreme and gets to hoist above their heads the most coveted trophy in amateur sports: The Golden Bowl.

While speed rules, it's impossible for an event to exist in Baltimore without a healthy dose of spectacle. Each year the racers get more elaborate and ridiculous: there has been a giant paper-maché unicorn that pooped rainbow streamers as it rolled towards the finish line, and a literal take on *Game of Thrones* which recreated the iron throne with a porcelain one surrounded by dozens of plungers, driven by a large bearded man dressed as the Mother of Dragons in a pink dress and long blond wig.

If your trip into Baltimore isn't during the weekend of the race, you'll still be able to take in some of the magic. Many of the racers are permanently displayed outside of Falkenhan's Hardware store (3401 Chestnut Avenue, Baltimore, MD 21211), and the official "Toilet Hall of Fame" can be viewed inside of Luigi's at (846 W 36th Street, Baltimore, MD 21211).

Address Hampdenfest, West 36th Street and Chestnut Avenue, Baltimore, MD 21211, www.hampdenfest.com | **Hours** Annual event | **Tip** Steve Baker is not just a toilet visionary, but also an accomplished artist whose exquisite stained-glass pieces can be seen all over Baltimore. Visit his Wholly Terra Studio (3406 Chestnut Avenue, Baltimore, MD 21211, www.whollyterra.com) to meet the man himself, and perhaps take a memorable piece of art for your own home.

99_Tochterman's Fishing Tackle

Gone fishin'

If you're a fisherman, you've probably already heard about Tochterman's, a century-old family-run establishment in Upper Fell's Point that's widely known as the best independent tackle shop in America. And if you have absolutely no interest in fishing whatsoever, you probably should hear about Tochterman's because they'll convert you. You don't get to stay open for over 100 years without being remarkable – or, for that matter, enthusiastic enough to convince just about anyone to pick up a pole and start fishing.

What began as a simple bait shop in 1916, has grown into a shrine to the sport. Fishing poles dramatically jut towards the ceiling atop the well-stocked shelves, laid out in winding rows that give Tochterman's the feel of a stately old-world labyrinth. This is the fishing store of choice for celebrities, politicians, and royalty (ask owner Tony Tochterman to tell you some stories). But if you were to ask about which customer generates the most excitement, it would be local legend Lefty Kreh, who bought his first fly rod here in 1948 and went on to become the top fly fisherman in the world. Ask Tony's wife Dee if Kreh was the king of all fishermen, and she will bluntly state, "Lefty Kreh is not king – he is God." Go Google him – the lady is most certainly correct.

Tochterman's still thrives on the mom-and-pop service you would have found in back in 1916. Every customer gets personal attention, and there's seemingly no question that can't be answered. Tony and Dee may equip the rich and famous, but they'll also help young kids buying their first poles, or the 30-something writer who walks in one afternoon with nary a clue about fishing. Every customer here is their most important customer, and that just might be enough to inspire you to grab a pole and set your status to "Gone Fishin'."

Address 1925 Eastern Avenue, Baltimore, MD 21231, +1 (410)327-6942 | **Hours** Mon – Fri 9am – 6pm, Sat 8am – 6pm | **Tip** The low-key Peter's Inn (504 S Ann Street, Baltimore, MD 21231, www.petersinn.com) screams "dive bar" upfront, but inside you'll find one of the most critically acclaimed restaurants in the entire city where the menu changes every week. No matter what you order, you won't be disappointed. Many local gourmands, including John Waters, cite Peter's as their favorite place in Baltimore to grab a bite.

100__ Under Armour At FX Studio

Sweatin' in the oldies

When the railroads and factories closed, Baltimore, like many major American cities, began a period of decline. Big businesses merged, banks consolidated, and eventually the thriving downtown district became a shadow of itself. Young entrepreneurs smelled opportunity. With affordable office space and a killer talent pool thanks to regional universities, many Internet companies, nonprofits, and creative studios seem to be popping up like wildflowers. Visionary entrepreneur Kevin Plank is a self-made man who began his billion-dollar company, Under Armour, out of the trunk of his car in the late 1990s. Today, the company name, as well as Plank himself, is synonymous with its second act: Plank has invested millions of dollars into infrastructure projects, new businesses, and real estate. One of his most stunning is the Under Armour Performance Center on the ground floor of 10 Light Street. From the street, it looks like an average sportswear shop. But the shop is merely the lobby of a gym so stunning you'd gladly work out there every day.

The building, originally the Baltimore Trust Company, was one of America's great art-deco skyscrapers and the tallest built outside of New York City, with soaring ornate windows, massive chandeliers, and gold-leaf embellishments. On the lower levels, FX Studios, a partnership between Plank and his former personal trainer, will take care of you from head to toe: working you out in the beautifully appointed gym, pampering you in the luxurious spa, and fancying you up in the downstairs salon. If you're not quite ready to leave, take a rest in what is likely the most interesting gym lounge you'll ever encounter: a luxuriously appointed 1920s bank vault. They have an "Under Armour Brand Only" rule for your workout gear. You can purchase what you need the shop; they're happy to lend you Under Armour shoes.

Address Bank of America Building, 10 Light Street, Baltimore, MD 21202, +1 (410)646-8272, www.fxstudios.com | Hours Mon–Fri 5:30am–10pm, Sat & Sun 7am–7pm | Tip You'll find one of America's first most influential monuments at 101 N Calvert Street: the Battle Monument, commemorating the infamous Battle of Baltimore in the War of 1812. Celebrating the common soldier over famous officers, it earned the town one of its earliest nicknames, "Monument City," and is the official emblem on the Baltimore flag.

101___Urology Museum
Yes, there's a museum for that

There are many museums of oddities sprinkled across the world, but it is quite difficult to think of one as remarkable as the National Museum of Urology. It is also quite difficult to find words to describe it at all, particularly ones that don't descend rapidly into sophomoric humor. It is, undoubtedly a must-see if you are in town, because even if your author cannot find words, you will most certainly have no shortage of things to say about this museum for the rest of your life.

Urology is the brand of medicine dedicated to the study both of the urinary tract and the functions of male genitalia. Situated in the lobby of the American Urological Association's national headquarters, this free museum will amaze, shock, and cause random involuntary spasms of cringing. A large permanent exhibition showcases many of the medical instruments used through the history of the field. It is worth it to try and arrange a private tour ahead of time to get the full and fascinating history behind each artifact.

A large gallery hosts a finely curated annual exhibition, which is created to travel to urology conferences across the country before being given an extended run back at headquarters. Past exhibits have focused on ancient history, early practices, and extreme medicine (these are all archived on their website if you'd care to look). Some of the more interesting artifacts from these exhibitions were subsequently donated by their owners to the museum's permanent collection, such as various early sex toys, Victorian anti-masturbation devices, exceptionally large kidney stones, and various foreign objects removed from the bladders of anonymous patients. There are no explanations given as to how those items got there in the first place, and perhaps it's better that way. However, if you'd like to find the answers to those questions, have a peek at their online gift shop.

Address 1000 Corporate Boulevard, Linthicum, MD 21090, +1 (410)689-3785, www.urologichistory.museum | **Hours** Mon–Fri 10am–5pm | **Tip** For something a little less intense, the nearby 1824 Benson-Hammond House (7101 Aviation Boulevard, Linthicum, MD 21090, www.aachs.org/benson-hammond-house), listed on the National Register of Historic Places, contains four period rooms and a small antique-doll museum.

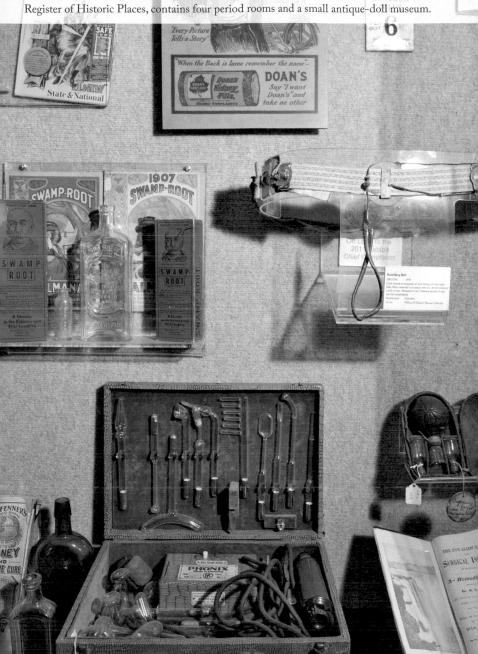

102__USS Torsk Sleepover
You won't get far walking in your sleep

The Inner Harbor is the city's biggest tourism draw, and it makes good use of its nautical past with the Historic Ships of Baltimore fleet: the sloop of war (and slave-ship interceptor) Constellation, the Pearl Harbor-veteran US Coast Guard Cutter Taney, the lightship Chesapeake, and the submarine USS Torsk. The average visitor buys tickets dockside and spends a pleasant day navigating the decks. A *brilliant* visitor assembles a group of friends to book a once in a lifetime experience: a sleepover on a World War II submarine.

This night is a full, hands-on experience where you'll go from swab to mate. You'll learn "usual submarine stuff": how they exist beneath the surface, how they navigate the depths of the sea, how to use a periscope, and, of course, everything you've ever wanted to know about torpedoes. You'll learn about all the action the Torsk has seen: how she earned her nickname "The Galloping Ghost of the Japanese Coast," how she fired the final torpedo of World War II, and how she set the all-time record for career dives: a whopping 11,844. And maybe, if you're lucky, you'll be able to see one of the Torsk's greatest claims to fame with your own eyes: the ghost of Joseph Grant Snow.

By all accounts, Joe Snow is a friendly ghost, just as he was in life. He was the quintessential all-American boy from small town Utah: high-school class president, varsity football star, intrepid Eagle Scout. Snow was a crewmember on the Torsk during WWII, and died not in combat but in a freak accident during a training dive when he was left topside, succumbing to the ocean as the Torsk dove beneath the waves. Ghost hunters have claimed they have seen his spirit wandering the deck, desperately clawing at the hatch, trying to get back in.

You'll be awakened at 6am, just like a real sailor, for a morning of fun before you return to your landlubbing lifestyle at 9am.

Address 501 E Pratt Street, Baltimore, MD 21202, +1 (410)539-1797, www.usstorsk.org |
Hours Daily 10am–4:30pm | **Tip** The exhibitions in the Reginald F Lewis African American
Museum celebrate over 400 years of black history, and should be required viewing for every
American (830 E Pratt Street, Baltimore, MD 21202, www.lewismuseum.org).

103_ Vagabond Players
The smell of the greasepaint, the roar of the crowd

For centuries, theater had been about spectacle: enormous sets, fabulous customers, and larger-than-life performances. With the advent of the cinema, spectacle seekers headed straight to the movie theater. This drastic shift necessitated dramatic changes in the theater that many artists had been quietly pushing for years. Playwrights toned down the melodrama and focused on strong narratives around relationships and social issues. Actors' performances gravitated from over-the-top to more restrained and natural. Budgets were stripped, scenery minimized, and theater itself became more intimate. The focus was now on art and creation over profit and commercialism: the Little Theater Movement was born.

In 1916, a small group of amateur players convened in the St. James Hotel to perform a one-act play by local literary giant H. L. Mencken. That was the first performance of the Vagabond Players, America's oldest continuously operating little theater company. Since that first performance, Baltimoreans have been introduced to other forms of entertainment – talking pictures, radio, professional sporting leagues, television, rock concerts, summer blockbusters, on-demand video, the Internet, smartphone streaming – and *still* the Vagabonds flourish.

What keeps the Vagabonds going is undying passion. This troupe has lasted for generations, continually attracting new artists to the stage and making them as passionate about the theater as their predecessors. In fact, that passion drove them for over 60 years before they found their permanent home in Fell's Point – this is a company that was truly made of vagabonds, performing in vacant storefronts, church basements, and buildings with no heat in the dead of winter. When you catch a show, you'll understand why they've persevered, and you'll be sure that they'll still be raising the curtain in another 100 years.

Address 806 S Broadway, Baltimore, MD 21231, +1 (410)563-9135,
www.vagabondplayers.org | Hours Check website for current performance schedule |
Tip You've probably noticed hundreds of bumper stickers in town that give one simple
command: "Eat Bertha's Mussels." You should probably listen to them and grab a bite
at Bertha's seafood restaurant just down the block (734 S Broadway, Baltimore,
MD 21231, www.berthas.com).

104_ Venice Tavern
Still celebrating the end of Prohibition

Back when Prohibition was repealed, folks couldn't wait to go back to the bar – but there were no bars to go to. But such a simple snafu could never stand in the way of folks looking to have a good time! Baltimoreans got to fixing things themselves by heading to their basements, fixing them up, and flinging open their doors. Who needs craft cocktails when you can enjoy the charm (and cheap beer) of a basement bar? Most such establishments have closed since the 1930s, but one stalwart hangs on: Highlandtown Venice Tavern.

For three generations, the DeSantis family has owned the tavern. The late Vince DeSantis, a second-generation owner with his brother Frank, continues to watches over the room as a portrait painted upon a slab of drywall that conceals the underside of a staircase. Behind the bar is a photo of President Franklin D. Roosevelt, who ended Prohibition in 1933, when the US Congress passed and ratified the 21st Amendment to the Constitution. The low drop grid ceiling still holds the faint scent of decades of cigarette smoke. If you made a habit of going there for a few decades, you'd know that, for the people who work here, this is not a "job." This is a family.

Venice Tavern is a joint that could make you feel like you've been transported to when the room would be filled with the sounds of men arguing in Italian, Polish, and German; back when there were no pretenses or mythologies built around the act of enjoying an ice-cold beer. There have been a few updates here and there, like the flat-panel television and the recent introduction of craft beers on tap, but even so, it feels like an anachronism.

Venice Tavern offers everything you could ever possibly want in a dive bar: the locals are friendly, the staff is friendly, and the beer is *cheap*. It's the type of place that can easily become a second home, the sort of place that could inspire you to move down the block just so you could stop in each night for a quick nip (or four).

Address 339 S Conkling Street, Baltimore, MD 21224, +1 (443)413-5647, www.facebook.com/venicetavern | Hours Daily 8am–2am | Tip One block south is the Highlandtown branch of the Enoch Pratt Public Library (3601 Eastern Avenue, Baltimore, MD 21224, www.prattlibrary.org/locations/southeast) over which peers a silver head affixed to a long pole. The head is that of Frank Zappa, music legend and professional weirdo who, of course, was a son of Baltimore.

105 The Walters Art Museum
Cabinet of curiosities for all to gaze upon

Before museums, there were "cabinets of curiosities." Nearly always existing in the exclusive realm of monarchs, aristocrats, and the absolutely filthy rich, these were massive collections of rarities and wonders the common man had never seen. These collections were a hodgepodge of categories, including natural history, archaeology, historical relics, priceless artwork, antiquities, and any other "curiosities" the collector fancied. If you want to go far back in time and imagine what it was like to have an extravagant collection fit for a king, head to Mount Vernon, where you can step into William and Henry Walters' Cabinet of Wonders.

William Walters made a fortune by investing in liquor, grain, banks, and railroads. Financially set for life, he turned his attention to art collecting after he fled to Europe during the Civil War. He returned to Baltimore at the war's conclusion and began collecting even more vigorously. He covered the walls of his Mount Vernon mansion with French landscapes, European modernism and exotic Asian art. His son Henry began collecting with him, eventually travelling the world on his father's behalf when he became too elderly to do so himself. It was Henry who expanded the collection from solely artwork to a full mélange of the fantastic: suits of armor, taxidermied beasts, fossils and gemstones, artifacts of ancient cultures, and rare manuscripts.

The mansion busting at the seams, Walters purchased the adjacent mansions on Charles Street and transformed them into a proper museum for the benefit of the public. Today the collection is carefully curated and organized by highly-educated experts, as befitting modern times. But if you turn left once you've climbed the grand marble staircase, you'll find the past preserved as it once was – an anachronistic museum inside of a museum, the likes of which you've never seen.

Address 600 N Charles Street, Baltimore, MD 21201, +1(410)547-9000, www.thewalters.org | Hours Wed & Fri–Sun 10am–5pm, Thu 10am–9pm | Tip You'll find another curiosity a block west: a building on top of which sits a large sculpture of Nipper, the iconic RCA dog (201 W Monument Street, Baltimore, MD 21201, www.mdhs.org), peering into the horn of the phonograph. That is the home of the Maryland Historical Society, which acquired the roadside icon after RCA changed its logo and retired ol' Nipper.

106 __ Westminster Hall Hauntings

The girl in the flowing white dress

Westminster Burying Ground is known as one of America's most haunted cemeteries. Incredibly, hometown hero Edgar Allan Po is not the most interesting resident of the cemetery.

When built in 1786 by the First Presbyterian Church, Westminster was a rural area a mile outside Baltimore. For the first wave of Baltimoreans, it was the most fashionable place to be buried – many names on the gravestones belong to the men after which the city's streets are named. 24 generals, 8 congressmen, 5 former mayors, and hundreds of veterans of both the American Revolution and the War of 1812 are buried here.

Baltimore began to expand rapidly, eventually placing this formerly pastoral setting in the middle of a bustling metropolis. In 1850, City Hall declared that any burial ground not attached to a church needed to be dug up and relocated outside of the city limits, an ordinance that the Presbyterians found unacceptable. Their solution was to build a church over existing graves, uprooting many bodies and moving them to unmarked graves, as well creating a system of catacombs underground. As the years passed, the bodies were subject to even more disturbances: body snatching for dissection at nearby Davidge Hall (see ch. 27), and years of neglect and vandalism.

The most commonly sighted ghost is Lucia Watson, a 16-year-old girl who died in 1816, often seen with long hair and a white flowing dress. Another is a nameless elderly woman who is seen walking up and down the pathways, possibly one of the displaced corpses searching for her body. Private tours can be arranged, where, if you're (un)lucky, you may run into Leona Wellesley, an infamous 19th-century lunatic who was so violent hope that she was buried in her straightjacket to contain her madness in the afterlife.

... In memory of
LUCIA WATSON
TAYLOR,
who died
February 7th. 1816,
aged 16 years.
Bless'd with
peculiar sweetness of temper
a mind pure and exalted,
a heart pious and faithful,
she died beloved and lamented.
Early bright transient chaste as morning dew
She sparkled was exhaled and went to Heaven

Address 519 W Fayette Street, Baltimore, MD 21201, +1 (410)706-2072,
www.westminsterhall.org | **Hours** Daily 8am–dusk | **Tip** The church, Westminster Hall,
has been desanctified and is now property of Johns Hopkins University, which uses it as
an event space and occasionally offers free lunchtime concerts featuring their restored
1882 pipe organ.

107 The Wire at Cylburn

Thin line between heaven and the arboretum

Baltimoreans have a love/hate relationship with television show *The Wire*. It is undoubtedly a masterpiece, heralded by many critics as the greatest television show ever that ought to add a new line. On the other hand, the portrait of the city's dark underbelly has become so synonymous with Baltimore that many outsiders believe that the entire city is a wasteland of lawlessness and danger. Like all cities, Baltimore has its fair share of problems, but there are many sides to this complicated metropolis, both positive and negative.

A moment that addresses the divide directly can be found in the episode "Final Grades," as gangbanger Bodie Broadus and cop Jimmy McNulty enjoy lunch together on a bench in Cylburn Arboretum. The park was originally the estate of a wealthy businessman whose Civil War-era mansion stands as the grounds' centerpiece. It remained a high-society residence until 1942, when it was sold to the City of Baltimore to be used as parkland. Connecting the historically aspirational Cylburn even closer to the have-nots, the mansion was turned into a home for neglected and abandoned children. The grounds were gradually planted, tilled, and transformed from a simple park into a full-fledged arboretum. Its mission is twofold: to teach young and old alike about the wonders of the natural world, and to create an oasis of natural beauty away from the stresses of city life. On *The Wire*, Bodie expresses shock over Cylburn, asking if they're still in the city.

It's a poignant moment. The dark world of *The Wire* exists only a mile from Cylburn's gates, yet it exists in a different America. The arboretum is serene and peaceful, and on a day with clear blue skies, it resembles a fictional version of heaven. It's easy in a place like this to forget your troubles – and Baltimore's. Though for a moment you can understand the distance between television and reality, the real issues that divide the city cannot be forgotten.

Address 4915 Greenspring Avenue, Baltimore, MD 21209, +1 (410)367-2217, www.cylburn.org | Hours Tue–Sun 8am–8pm, closed on federal holidays | Tip Cylburn Arboretum is known as a top spot for birdwatching, and one of the favorite location of the Baltimore Bird Club, which periodically offers free bird walks. Visit www.baltimorebirdclub.org for all the insider secrets of birding at the arboretum.

108 __ Wockenfuss Candies
Five generations of confection perfection

No trip to, well, *anywhere* is complete without seeking out at least one candy shop, and Baltimore is lucky to have more than its fair share. Mary Sue Chocolates has been cracking out chocolate bars and Easter eggs since 1948. Rheb's is still making candy out of the row-house basement they began in back in 1917 – and still selling out of their tiny shop that started off as their garage. Goetze's is still cranking out caramels in East Baltimore as they have been since 1895. Up north on Harford Road, however, is a place that's not only been making chocolates and candies for over 100 years, but they've also kept this sanctuary of sweetness in the family.

It all started with great-great-grandpa Herman Charles Wockenfuss, who arrived in Baltimore from Prussia in 1885. He worked as a candy maker, eventually striking out on his own and establishing the Wockenfuss Candy Company in 1915. After World War II, his son Herman joined the family business. Alongside the baby boom there was a sort of "candy boom," as servicemen were returning from overseas with a taste for European chocolates and rich, creamy caramels. The company updated its equipment in the 1950s to keep up with surging demand, including an enrobing machine where truffle fillings ride down a conveyor belt through a waterfall of chocolate. But much of the candy is made by hand as it was in the old days. Fudge is still made by confectionary experts in large copper kettles where the mixture is stirred at just the right intervals to create the finest sugar crystals, which results in superior textures. The recipes haven't changed much in the past 100 years. Why mess with perfection?

Candy making is not merely cooking – it takes a special kind of genius to create confectionary alchemy. With the fifth generation now entering the business, the gene for that genius is an essential part of the Wockenfuss DNA.

Address 6831 Harford Road, Baltimore, MD 21234, +1 (410)483-4414,
www.wockenfusscandies.com | Hours Mon – Sat 8am – 6pm, special hours for Mother's
Day | Tip When Clementine Restaurant shuttered in 2015, locals were so heartbroken
that they helped the owner raise $8,000 through an online fundraiser to reopen. Now
they're back and better than ever, serving a rotating menu of farm-to-table specials and
a brunch that people travel miles to enjoy (5402 Harford Road, Baltimore, MD 21214,
www.clementinebaltimore.com).

109 __ Woman's Industrial Exchange

Sleepless in Baltimore

Hollywood has given us thousands of romantic comedies, but few that stick with us like the 1993 Nora Ephron classic, *Sleepless in Seattle*. This is the film that made Tom "America's Dad" Hanks and Meg "the Girl Next Door" Ryan one of cinema's most iconic film duos. That classic final scene in New York City and the film's title make most people forget that the majority of the film took place in Charm City.

Some of the most lovely scenery featured was during the scenes between Annie and her best friend Becky (played by Rosie O'Donnell), as they ambled around the Mount Vernon neighborhood discussing the story they'd heard on the radio. On the corner of Charles Street and West Pleasant Street, you'll find the Woman's Industrial Exchange, an unassuming building with a storied history that played a significant role in the film.

Built in 1815, it became an economic haven for women after the Civil War, many of whom were now widowed or wives of men who had been gravely injured and could no longer work. It was not yet "acceptable" for women to work, so the Exchange gave them a place to sell their handiwork discreetly. A tearoom was opened in the late 19th century, which gave women even more employment opportunities. It was open for well over 100 years, and Nora Ephron fell in love with it as she was scouting locations for the film. She ate lunch there daily and decided to include it in a scene where Annie and Becky have lunch. She felt the building's timeless quality would keep the film relevant for years to come. The woman who plays the server in that scene wasn't an actress, but rather had been a longtime waitress for the Exchange. She was given a few lines, which she rejected, saying "look, just let me do it my way." She claimed that after working the role for real for 45 years she sort of knew what she was doing, and Ephron agreed.

Address 333 N Charles Street, Baltimore, MD 21201, +1 (410)685-4388, www.womansindustrialexchange.org | Hours Currently viewable from the outside only | Tip Many sights in Baltimore will delight *Sleepless in Seattle* fans. There's the Brooks Robinson statue outside of Camden Yards – the player Annie mentions in her letter that wins the heart of widower Sam's young son Jonah. Head to Fell's Point to see Annie's apartment (904 S Broadway, Baltimore, MD 21231), and then walk south to the water to stroll along the pier where she sat one night to evaluate her ill-fated engagement to Walter.

110 Woodlawn Vase

Preakness Stakes Pimlico prize

On the third Sunday of every May, horseracing fans meet at Pimlico Race Course for the Preakness Stakes, the second leg of the Triple Crown. The victor and rider enjoy a moment to hold the most storied, and most valuable, trophy in American sports: The Woodlawn Vase.

Valued at over four million dollars, the vase was forged out of solid silver as a "challenge cup" by Tiffany & Co for the Woodlawn Race Course in Louisville, Kentucky in 1861. During the Civil War, the vase was buried to prevent it from being melted down for ammunition. The championship horse whose likeness adorns the top of the vase also went into hiding, for fear he would be drafted into battle. That stallion, Lexington, sired another champion stud, whose name, Preakness, would become inseparable from the vase.

After the war, the vase became the championship trophy of Churchill Downs, home of the Kentucky Derby, the first leg of the Triple Crown. In 1878 the vase was won by a horse owned by the Dwyer brothers, two butchers from Brooklyn and the most successful stable owners of the era. The vase would be contested for at various racetracks in the New York area for the next 40 years. Its last stop was the Belmont Stakes, the final leg of the Triple Crown.

In 1917, the Woodlawn Vase was gifted to the Maryland Jockey Club, soon becoming the championship trophy of the Preakness Stakes. Due to its value not just in dollars, but as the true uniter of the Triple Crown, it was decided that winners would receive a two-thirds-size replica, with the vase permanently residing under heavy protection on Maryland soil. Its home is in the English Sporting Art Gallery of the Baltimore Museum of Art, which it leaves but one day a year with white-gloved soldiers of the Army National Guard, to grace a new champion joining the short list of those who have ever won the most exceptional trophy in sports.

Address 10 Art Museum Drive, Baltimore, MD 21218-3898, +1 (443)573-1700, www.artbma.org | Hours Wed–Sun 10am–5pm | Tip The BMA is also home to one of the earliest, and most important, collections of African art in the country, with works spanning from ancient Egypt to contemporary pieces.

111__Zissimos Bar

True comedic success is no laughing matter

Baltimore was a major stop on the vaudeville circuits of the early 20th century. Crowds flocked to the regal Hippodrome Theater to see legends like Jack Benny and Bob Hope. Around the corner was another, lesser theater: The Palace, the Baltimore arm of the infamous Minksy's Burlesque. While the big names played a block south, second-rate joke men worked the burlesque circuit for peanuts, hoping they'd one day get their shot on the nicer stage.

One such comedian was Lou Costello, a former boxer and failed actor. He began to perform in burlesque sketches in 1930, the same year his aunt Eva Zissimopoulis and her husband Atha opened Zissimos Bar on the ground floor of their Hampden home. He toured incessantly, struggling as any small-time, aspiring comedian does. Every time the burlesque circuit would take him to The Palace, he would spend time at aunt Eva's place.

One night in 1936, Costello's usual partner fell ill before a major gig at New York City's Eltinge Theater. Another comic, William Alexander "Bud" Abbott, was brought in to replace him, and the comedic chemistry between the impromptu duo made them an immediate success. They began working together exclusively from that point on, from burlesque, to vaudeville, to Hollywood. (They even played the Hippodrome several times!)

Even though he was finally a star, Costello still came to Zissimos whenever he'd pass through Baltimore. His visits became massive neighborhood affairs, and the bar would be packed. He was always the life of the party – tap dancing, juggling, telling jokes, and handing out dollar bills.

Over 80 years later, the bar remains in the family, and their legacy of hilarity continues. That same upstairs apartment where Costello spent many nights is currently the home of the Charm City Comedy Project, showcasing the next generation of comedic geniuses.

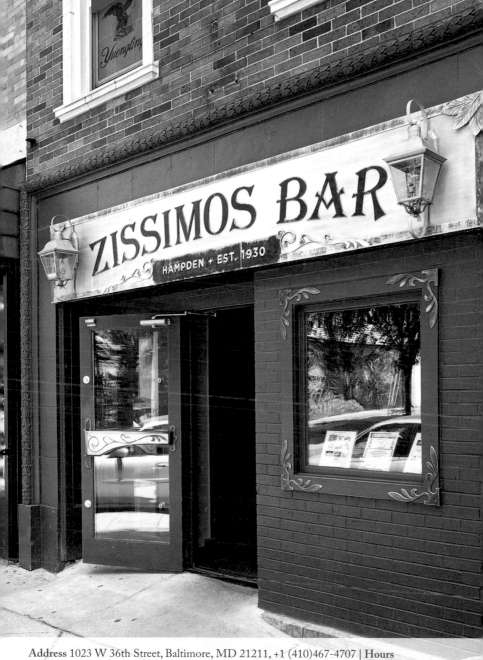

Address 1023 W 36th Street, Baltimore, MD 21211, +1 (410)467-4707 | **Hours**
Mon–Wed 9am–2am, Thu–Sun 6am–2am | **Tip** The home of the Maryland Society
for the Protection of Animals (SPCA) is hidden from view streetside, which is why
only animal lovers know that it's housed in a Civil War-era mansion (3300 Falls Road,
Baltimore, MD 21211, www.mdspca.org). The grounds are expansive and, as you can
imagine, very dog friendly.

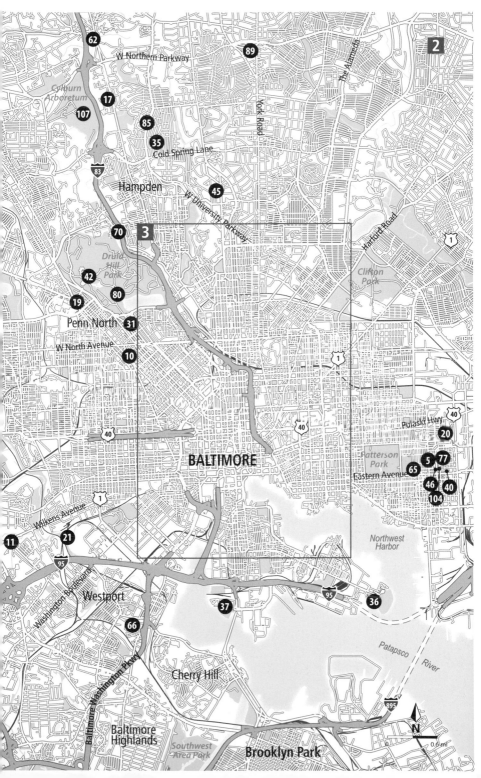

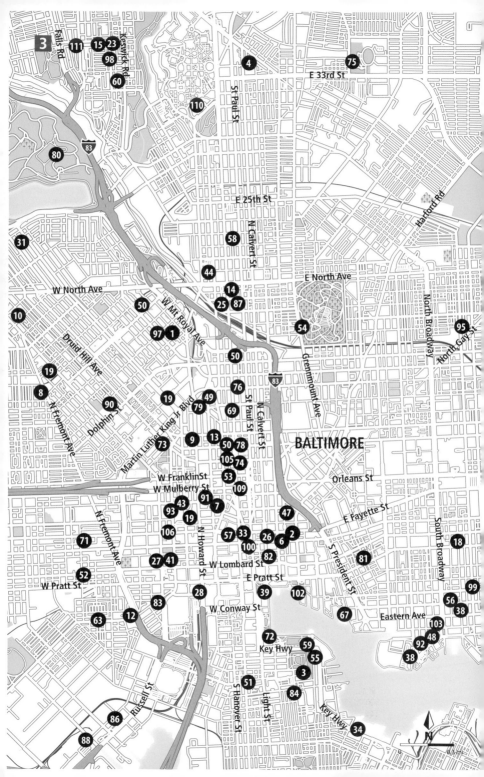

Lucia Jay von Seldeneck,
Carolin Huder, Verena Eidel
**111 PLACES IN BERLIN
THAT YOU SHOULDN'T MISS**
ISBN 978-3-95451-208-9

Rüdiger Liedtke
**111 PLACES IN MUNICH
THAT YOU SHOULDN'T MISS**
ISBN 978-3-95451-222-5

Frank McNally
**111 PLACES IN DUBLIN
THAT YOU SHOULDN'T MISS**
ISBN 978-3-95451-649-0

Rike Wolf
**111 PLACES IN HAMBURG
THAT YOU SHOULDN'T MISS**
ISBN 978-3-95451-234-8

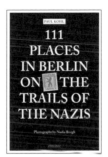

Paul Kohl
**111 PLACES IN BERLIN
ON THE TRAIL OF THE NAZIS**
ISBN 978-3-95451-323-9

Peter Eickhoff
**111 PLACES IN VIENNA
THAT YOU SHOULDN'T MISS**
ISBN 978-3-95451-206-5

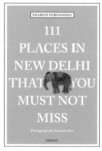

Sharon Fernandes
**111 PLACES IN NEW DELHI
THAT YOU MUST NOT MISS**
ISBN 978-3-95451-648-3

Sally Asher, Michael Murphy
**111 PLACES IN NEW ORLEANS
THAT YOU MUST NOT MISS**
ISBN 978-3-95451-645-2

Gordon Streisand
**111 PLACES IN MIAMI
AND THE KEYS
THAT YOU MUST NOT MISS**
ISBN 978-3-95451-644-5

Dirk Engelhardt
111 PLACES IN BARCELONA
THAT YOU MUST NOT MISS
ISBN 978-3-95451-353-6

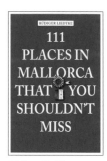

Rüdiger Liedtke
111 PLACES ON MALLORCA
THAT YOU SHOULDN'T MISS
ISBN 978-3-95451-281-2

Marcus X. Schmid
111 PLACES IN ISTANBUL
THAT YOU MUST NOT MISS
ISBN 978-3-95451-423-6

Stefan Spath
111 PLACES IN SALZBURG
THAT YOU SHOULDN'T MISS
ISBN 978-3-95451-230-0

Ralf Nestmeyer
111 PLACES IN PROVENCE
THAT YOU MUST NOT MISS
ISBN 978-3-95451-422-9

Christiane Bröcker,
Babette Schröder
111 PLACES IN STOCKHOLM
THAT YOU MUST NOT MISS
ISBN 978-3-95451-459-5

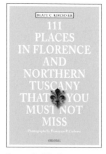

Beate C. Kirchner
111 PLACES IN FLORENCE
AND NORTHERN TUSCANY
THAT YOU MUST NOT MISS
ISBN 978-3-95451-613-1

Floriana Petersen, Steve Werney
111 PLACES IN SAN FRANCISCO
THAT YOU MUST NOT MISS
ISBN 978-3-95451-609-4

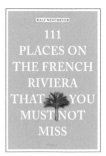

Ralf Nestmeyer
111 PLACES ON THE
FRENCH RIVIERA
THAT YOU MUST NOT MISS
ISBN 978-3-95451-612-4

Gerd Wolfgang Sievers
111 PLACES IN VENICE
THAT YOU MUST NOT MISS
ISBN 978-3-95451-460-1

Petra Sophia Zimmermann
111 PLACES IN VERONA
AND LAKE GARDA THAT
YOU MUST NOT MISS
ISBN 978-3-95451-611-7

Rüdiger Liedtke,
Laszlo Trankovits
111 PLACES IN CAPE TOWN
THAT YOU MUST NOT MISS
ISBN 978-3-95451-610-0

Gillian Tait
111 PLACES IN EDINBURGH
THAT YOU SHOULDN'T MISS
ISBN 978-3-95451-883-8

Laurel Moglen, Julia Posey
111 PLACES IN LOS ANGELES
THAT YOU SHOULDN'T MISS
ISBN 978-3-95451-884-5

Giulia Castelli Gattinara,
Mario Verin
111 PLACES IN MILAN
THAT YOU MUST NOT MISS
ISBN 978-3-95451-331-4

John Sykes
111 PLACES IN LONDON
THAT YOU SHOULDN'T MISS
ISBN 978-3-95451-346-8

Julian Treuherz,
Peter de Figueiredo
111 PLACES IN LIVERPOOL
THAT YOU SHOULDN'T MISS
ISBN 978-3-95451-769-5

Jo-Anne Elikann
111 PLACES IN NEW YORK
THAT YOU MUST NOT MISS
ISBN 978-3-95451-052-8

Matěj Černý, Marie Peřinová
**111 PLACES IN PRAGUE
THAT YOU SHOULDN'T MISS**
ISBN 978-3-7408-0144-1

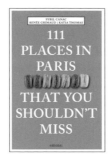

Sybil Canac, Renée Grimaud,
Katia Thomas
**111 PLACES IN PARIS THAT
YOU SHOULDN'T MISS**
ISBN 978-3-7408-0159-5

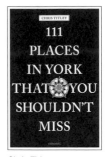

Chris Titley
**111 PLACES IN YORK THAT
YOU SHOULDN'T MISS**
ISBN 978-3-95451-768-8

Kathrin Bielfeldt,
Raymond Wong, Jürgen Bürger
**111 PLACES IN HONG KONG
THAT YOU SHOULDN'T MISS**
ISBN 978-3-95451-936-1

Kirstin von Glasow
**111 COFFEESHOPS IN
LONDON THAT YOU MUST
NOT MISS**
ISBN 978-3-95451-614-8

Mark Gabor, Susan Lusk
**111 SHOPS IN NEW YORK
THAT YOU MUST NOT MISS**
ISBN 978-3-95451-351-2

Kirstin von Glasow
**111 SHOPS IN LONDON
THAT YOU SHOULDN'T MISS**
ISBN 978-3-95451-341-3

Desa Philadelphia
**111 SHOPS IN LOS ANGELES
THAT YOU MUST NOT MISS**
ISBN 978-3-95451-615-5

Aylie Lonmon
**111 SHOPS IN MILAN
THAT YOU MUST NOT MISS**
ISBN 978-3-95451-637-7

Acknowledgments

There are far too many people to credit than these pages will allow, so if you don't see your name here but feel you should have been included, just give yourself a pat on the back. I must definitely thank my amazing husband Matt who is my partner in everything I do (this book included). Even greater thanks go to our sons Atticus and Toby who didn't complain as much as I expected as I dragged them around Baltimore for months on end exploring, and were mostly understanding about the fact that their mother almost always had her head buried in her laptop. Without Veronica Weiss, I would not be able to function as a working mom, so thank you for being the queen of my village. Thank you to my wonderful and patient editor Karen Seiger, and my darling Rhonda Kave for suggesting this book happen in the first place. And all my love to all the people who told me stories and pointed me in so many exciting directions, and who welcomed us home with open arms: Nick & Nikki, Erika and Aman, David & Laura Alima, Larry Hankin, Kelly Taylor, Steve Baker, Will Cocks, L Drew Pumphrey, Aimee Harmon-Darrow, Dave Seel, Summer Cullen, Kevin Lynch, Kit Waskom Pollard, Kathy Harvey, John Makowski, Rebecca Murphy, John Dean, Dara Bunjon, Marisa Dobson, Jennifer Waldera, Traci Mathena, Lisa Bleich, Marissa Canino, Latrice Brown, Krystal Chastain, the Enoch Pratt Public Library, Explore Baltimore, the dozens of community organizations that keep this city vibrant and moving forward, all of the wonderful servers, salespeople and other members of the working class who were kind and helpful while I was scoping them out incognito (surprise!), and all the wonderful people of Baltimore that I haven't met yet (we're going to be friends soon – I promise).
– *Allison Robicelli*

Thank you to Pam Li from Johns Hopkins Magazine for recommending me to my editor, Karen Seiger, whose enthusiasm for the book was infectious. Allison Robicelli inspired me to revisit old favorites and discover new ones. D. Edward Vogel of Bengies was very welcoming, even if the signs forbidding photography in his drive-in scared me a little. John Waters, thank you so much for your support of this project. I hope to see you again soon at Club Charles.
Deepest thanks to Penny Forester for her critical eye and excellent organizational skills. I've relied on her for over 15 years to deliver the best of every shoot.
– *John Dean*

The author

Allison Robicelli is an author, chef, entrepreneur, and backyard adventurer. She is the author of the critically acclaimed cookbook *Robicelli's: A Love Story, With Cupcakes*, and has written for Food52, Eater, Saveur, Food Network and more. A lifelong aficionado of municipal history, she has a passion for treating cities as playgrounds, unearthing hidden treasures and seeking out untold stories. Born and raised in New York City, she was drawn to Baltimore for its creative spirit, impeccable architecture, robust culture and vibrant communities. She lives with her husband, two children and three cats in Baltimore's most charmingly titled neighborhood: Pigtown.

The photographer

John Dean is a freelance photographer and video producer, who specializes in photographing people in different environments. He was given a Brownie 620 box camera when he was 7 years old, and he has been hooked ever since. He calls himself an mateur in the literal sense that he loves photography all the doors it has opened for him. He is happy to be working in the current "golden age" of high definition documentary film making, producing videos for the past 15 years for museums and non-profit organizations.